# Praise for *Stand Back and Deliver*

"In *Stand Back and Deliver*, the authors provide strong, practical guidance on how to leverage the strengths of your entire team to get the right job done. Their experience in the trenches shines through with clear examples of how their approach can be applied to make your projects successful, regardless of the domain."

**—Jim Brosseau, author of Software Teamwork: Taking Ownership for Success**

"A book rich with content, practical tools that can be easily adopted, and great examples that relate to the common workplace!"

**—Lisa Shoop, software director at Sabre Holdings**

"For those new to project management, *Stand Back and Deliver* offers the voice of experience. Its message is clear: Understand the value you must deliver, understand and manage the project's complexity, trust in your people, and above all, have the courage to do the right thing."

**—Patrick Bailey, Department of Computer Science and Information Systems, Calvin College**

"With most business books I am happy if I learn one or two key things that I want to put to use. This book is full of such concepts and tools and provides enough detail and examples that I'm confident I'd not just want to use them but would be able to do so successfully."

**—Terri Pitcher, IT manager**

"Today's postmodern organizational environment requires a new approach, and this book will provide many insights to the reader. You will learn how to detach and stand back, and yet passionately engage and deliver."

**—Greg Githens, managing partner at Catalyst Management Consulting, LLC**

D1311801

# Stand Back and Deliver

# STAND BACK AND DELIVER

## ACCELERATING BUSINESS AGILITY

**Pollyanna Pixton**
**Niel Nickolaisen**
**Todd Little**
**Kent McDonald**

*Illustrations by Jim Lewis*

✦Addison-Wesley

Upper Saddle River, NJ • Boston • Indianapolis • San Francisco
New York • Toronto • Montreal • London • Munich • Paris • Madrid
Capetown • Sydney • Tokyo • Singapore • Mexico City

Many of the designations used by manufacturers and sellers to distinguish their products are claimed as trademarks. Where those designations appear in this book, and the publisher was aware of a trademark claim, the designations have been printed with initial capital letters or in all capitals.

The authors and publisher have taken care in the preparation of this book, but make no expressed or implied warranty of any kind and assume no responsibility for errors or omissions. No liability is assumed for incidental or consequential damages in connection with or arising out of the use of the information or programs contained herein.

The publisher offers excellent discounts on this book when ordered in quantity for bulk purchases or special sales, which may include electronic versions and/or custom covers and content particular to your business, training goals, marketing focus, and branding interests. For more information, please contact:

U.S. Corporate and Government Sales
(800) 382-3419
corpsales@pearsontechgroup.com

For sales outside the United States please contact:

International Sales
international@pearson.com

Visit us on the Web: informit.com/aw

*Library of Congress Cataloging-in-Publication Data*

Stand back and deliver: accelerating business agility / Pollyanna Pixton ... [et al.].
    p.    cm.
  Includes index.
  ISBN 978-0-321-57288-2 (pbk. : alk. paper)
  1. Leadership.  I. Pixton, Pollyanna.

HD57.7.S716 2009
658.4'092—dc22

                                        2009012654

Pearson Education, Inc.
Rights and Contracts Department
501 Boylston Street, Suite 900
Boston, MA 02116
Fax (617) 671-3447

ISBN-13: 978-0-321-57288-2
ISBN-10:    0-321-57288-2

Text printed in the United States on recycled paper at Courier in Stoughton, Massachusetts.
First printing, June 2009

# CONTENTS

# PREFACE

The past few years have seen the rapid ascent of technology in the workplace. Enterprise applications have gone from supporting business applications to facilitating customer management, business intelligence, and social networks. Networks have evolved from being closed to the wired Internet to ubiquitous wireless connectivity. Each time technology advances, a corresponding change in business models and opportunities occurs. These changing business models then fuel the need for new technologies.

The pace of this technology/business model innovation is accelerating. In the face of such a dynamic marketplace, it is easy to feel overwhelmed as we sort through all that we must do not just to keep pace, but to get—and stay—ahead of the competition and the changes. We can find ourselves spending our days buried by things to do and tasks to complete, yet still not accomplishing the things that matter most—defining and delivering a sustainable competitive advantage and ensuring that we make real progress every day.

## Who Should Read This Book?

If you are in a leadership position—the leader of an organization, the leader of a team, or the leader of a project—this book is intended for you. As you learn about the tools and read stories about how they have been applied to a wide range of situations, think through how you might apply these tools to the situations, issues, and opportunities you face. You can apply these tools immediately in your organization, with your team, and for your project. They are intended to help you unleash the talent that resides in your teams and organizations. The tools will help you figure out where you should focus your time, attention, and resources. In addition, they will help you assess risk and identify ways to manage the complexity and uncertainty of your initiatives. The tools will also help you make decisions based on a variety of inputs—not just estimated costs and benefits. Finally, the tools will help you work through your role as a leader in a dynamic environment and organization, becoming a more effective leader in the process.

## Why Stand Back and Deliver?

We chose the title *Stand Back and Deliver* for this book because it concisely points out the key message of the book: You need to involve all the right players in the organization to effectively deliver a sustained competitive advantage. Effectively involving all the key players requires leaders to stand back and let those best suited for a particular initiative or decision come forward and take responsibility for delivering the right solutions. Standing back does not imply abdicating all responsibility, but rather requires leaders to perform a careful balancing act between stepping back to let the right people in the organization do their thing and stepping up to provide steering when the team has strayed off course.

We chose "deliver" as part of the book title because delivery is the ultimate measure of success. Put simply, did the team actually deliver value to the business? No other measure of success is important. It is irrelevant how well the team followed a certain methodology if its results didn't add value to the organization. Because we are pragmatic and focused on value, we see delivery—what you accomplish—as being much more important than methodology—how you got there.

## What Influences Our Thinking?

The influences on our thoughts have been many and varied. Here are the major precepts that guide our thinking:

- **The answers are in the organization.** The people who best understand the problems an organization faces and know the best way to solve them are the people who are already part of the organization. They have not solved the problems already because they have not been given the opportunity to do so. Our tools are focused on identifying those answers hidden inside the organization.

- **Pragmatic answers are the best.** We are much more interested in doing what works than doing something just for the sake of doing it. The former tactic often seems much too difficult. We are also interested in doing what works even if it is different from the accepted practices and methods. Common sense is sometimes preferred to common practice.
- **If you don't absolutely need to do something, don't do it.** You can call that attitude "being a slacker"; we prefer to call it "being efficient." Organizations typically have too much to do, so we look for strategies that encourage organizations to get more done by doing less. The key is to focus on the most important tasks and treat the tasks according to the value they create.
- **Do what works best for your situation.** There is no best practice that applies equally well across the board. There will always be approaches that work better in some situations than in others. Always look to understand your situation and select the best approaches. Remember, the answer to all questions is, ultimately, "It depends."
- **We are not offering a silver bullet.** Because of our last stated belief, we cannot in good conscience tell you that there is no best practice and then turn around and say, "Well, except for our tools, which will work *all* the time." If you are looking for a silver bullet in this book, you will be disappointed.
- Finally, and most importantly, **none of these tools will work when people work in isolation.** All of the tools rely on having people with different backgrounds, experiences, and skill sets from across the organization work together to do what is right for the organization.

## How We Wrote This Book

The authors of this book are a perfect example of a distributed team: Pollyanna and Niel live in Salt Lake City, Utah; Todd lives in Houston, Texas; and Kent lives in Des Moines, Iowa. We weren't lucky enough to be able to work on the book full time, because we all have "day jobs." As a consequence, we had to find unique ways to make progress on the book when it wasn't our only responsibility and when we couldn't work in the same room at the same time.

To make up for the distributed nature of our writing team, we tried to find as many opportunities as we could to get together for a day or two at a time to discuss the big themes of the book and the objective for writing it. In between those times, each of us took responsibility for a chapter or two, which we would draft and then share with the rest of the team for editing and feedback. Some chapters were easier to write than others. We also found out that we were much more effective when we all met in the same room to discuss issues than when we tried to resolve disagreements via email. Our experiences should come as no surprise to anyone who has ever worked on a distributed team. Email hides so many communication channels that can exacerbate disagreements and hinder collaboration. We worked remote from one another because we had to—but if we had our preference, we would have written the entire book with all of us in the same room.

# ACKNOWLEDGMENTS

## Pollyanna Pixton

I was fortunate to be supported and encouraged by many wonderful people: Byron Russell, Chris Matts, Sue McKinney, Imogene and Mike Rigdon, Lyn and Russell Taylor, Barbara O'Brian and Kathy Elton, Tim Shultz, Carol Osborn, and Denise Wojtowicz.

I want to thank Jim Highsmith for bringing me along in the agile community and Mary Poppendieck for her guidance and friendship as I discovered my ideas and began to put them to work to create better leaders. I would also like to thank Lee Copland and the people at SQE who gave me a forum to talk about these ideas. FFKR Architects has been a wonderful organization where we put these tools to real work.

I want to thank my coauthors Kent and Todd for their friendship and work in finding the best ways to express our thoughts. I especially want to thank Niel Nickolaisen, who has been a wonderful friend and, for five years, has never wavered about the value of our ideas. I am lucky to know someone who has always had my growth as his best interest.

## Niel Nickolaisen

First of all, I want to thank my close friends and coauthors from whom I have learned so much. If Pollyanna had not involved me in her work on collaborative leadership and introduced me to Todd and Kent, I would never have participated in writing this—or any—book. Beyond my coauthors, there are way too many people whom I should thank to list here— from Mike Loundes, the best boss I ever had, to Kirk Benson, the person from whom I have learned the most about leadership and business.

# Todd Little

I would like to thank and acknowledge many of my friends, coworkers, and mentors during my time at Halliburton/Landmark Graphics and predecessor companies Western Atlas Software and J. S. Nolen and Associates. In particular, I was fortunate to work with David Archer, Richard Kendall, and Steve Webb, who were excellent at demonstrating and executing "stand back and deliver" leadership. I would also like to acknowledge my colleagues who helped develop the Context Leadership Model: Forrest Greene, Tessy Phillips, Rex Pilger, Robert Poldervaart, and Karl Zachry. Ahsan Rahi and Prakash Roopani engaged me in many thought-provoking discussions, and Ahsan's experience applying the models to an oil field service provider confirmed that these approaches have applicability well beyond software development. Karen Wiley and Liz Broussard have been my pillars of strength, and have always been there to support me.

Many leaders in the agile software development community have been amazingly supportive: Mary and Tom Poppendieck, Ken Schwaber, Mike Cohn, and many others. I have enjoyed many fun times with Tim Lister, and his work with Tom DeMarco on peopleware and risk management has had a big influence on my approach to leadership. Jim Highsmith must be singled out for his leadership in founding the APLN, and for encouraging me to become involved in its founding and in the drafting of the Declaration of Interdependence for Agile Project Leadership.

Lastly, I would like to thank Alistair Cockburn for being willing to listen to some crazy ideas about building a conference and a community, and for giving me the opportunity to be a part of building that community. Alistair's work with the Crystal approach to software development was also an important building block for our work on applying context to project leadership. It was also through Alistair that I happened to meet Pollyanna, and through these connections in the agile community I eventually met Niel and Kent. Perhaps the most important way that Alistair influenced me was, when given a choice of two alternatives, he suggested that we spend our time one evening at dinner with Pollyanna rather than attend a geeky software user group. It has been a constant flow of new thoughts and ideas ever since.

## Kent McDonald

Thanks to my friends and coauthors Niel, Todd, and Pollyanna for being so generous with their knowledge, advice, and support. I have learned so much in the past four years as a result of working with all of you. A special thanks to Jim Highsmith, who provided me with the path into the agile community through which I had the chance to get to know my coauthors.

Thanks to Chris Matts for being an endless source of new ideas and practical insights. Thanks to Greg Goodman for being a sounding board on matters of all kinds, be it this book or other things. Thanks to Cinda Voegtli, Teresa Fenton, and all the others too numerous to mention who have given me the opportunities to refine, expand, and share my ideas through their practical application.

Finally, thanks to my wife, Beth McDonald, for her support and perseverance during the writing process, and to my parents, Barb and Ivan McDonald, and my in-laws, Fred and Lorie Grau, for all of your help.

## Joint Acknowledgments

Even though four of us took on the task of writing this book, many more people were involved in the process of its development. Thanks especially to those who took early looks at our drafts and provided much-needed feedback: Lynne Billing, Jim Brosseau, Greg Githens, Jim Highsmith, Hannu Kokko, Sue McKinney, Terri Pitcher, Tom Poppendieck, Michele Sliger, and Cinda Voegtli.

Thanks also to Chris Guzikowski, Raina Chrobak, and the rest of the crew at Addison-Wesley for all of your help and cat herding during the entire writing and production process.

Finally, a very special thank you to Jim Lewis, who stepped up and delivered the great illustrations in the book. He did a fantastic job of capturing our ideas just as they might be drawn during a conversation about them. We are grateful for his contribution.

# About the Authors

Everyone looks at the world through a series of filters, which differ based on our backgrounds and experiences. The four of us are no exception, and our filters have influenced the way we share these leadership tools. To help you understand our perspectives and determine why you should care what we have to say, we thought we would give you a little insight into our backgrounds.

**Pollyanna Pixton** is an international collaborative leadership expert who has developed models for collaboration and collaborative leadership throughout her thirty-eight years of working inside and consulting with corporations and organizations. Pollyanna helps leaders create companies where talent and innovation are unleashed—making them more productive, efficient, and profitable. She was primarily responsible for leading the development of the Swiss electronic stock exchange. In addition, she has developed control systems for electrical power plants throughout the world and merged the technologies and data systems of large financial institutions.

**Niel Nickolaisen** started his career in engineering, but then got involved with process improvement methods such as Lean and Six Sigma. The need to improve processes soon pulled him into managing large, put-the-business-at-risk IT projects and then IT leadership. Niel has a passion for focusing and aligning teams and organizations, and for finding ways to reduce both process and system complexity. His motto is, "Let's do more smart stuff and less stupid stuff."

**Todd Little** is a chemical engineer turned petroleum engineer who has been developing software products for more than thirty years. For more than twenty years, he has led teams and groups of teams in keeping the focus on delivering results on a regular basis. Todd has been quite active in the agile software development movement, as it is well aligned with his own observations about the importance of proper attention to purpose, people, and process in "making ship happen."

**Kent McDonald** has nearly fifteen years of experience as a project and program manager in a variety of industries, ranging from automotive to financial services. Throughout those various projects, he has always striven to keep his team's focus on the purpose of the project, avoiding where possible extraneous activities that do not add any value to the completion of the project. Kent has observed that properly aligned projects that follow the right approach and utilize collaboration are usually the most effective and add the most value to the organization.

# CHAPTER 1

# INTRODUCTION TO KEY PRINCIPLES

In this chapter, we explain what we mean by "stand back and deliver" by first presenting some situations that may seem alarmingly familiar to you. We then cover some of our core concepts and beliefs that underlie the tools we recommend you implement to get your organization going in the right direction.

## What Could Go Wrong?

Have you ever done things by the book, but the book was out of print? Such was the case for a large, successful product company. This company had developed what it considered to be a revolutionary new product. With its heavy engineering background, the company did product development by the book—the way it had worked many times before.

Through its research and development activities, the company had discovered that it could use a waste material as the basic raw material for a new product. Imagine the possibilities: Currently the company pays to dispose of this material, but now it could use this "waste material" to make an industrial product. The company did what it had always done. It selected one of its best engineers to sort through the product design and manufacturing options. It set up the engineer with all of the development and testing equipment he would need. It gave the engineer the time and flexibility he needed to design what he thought the market needed.

Within a year, the engineer had perfected a formulation that worked. The resulting product had impressive characteristics. It had high workability and could be formed into various shapes and sizes. The engineer produced small batches of the product that the company used to generate early customer interest. Using these small batches, the company formed several industry joint ventures and alliances. The future looked bright.

The engineer next worked on the manufacturing processes needed to produce the product. In parallel with this effort, the company issued press releases and featured the new product in its annual report: "Coming soon, a revolutionary, green product." One year later, the engineer announced that his work was done. He documented the product formulation. He described in great detail how to scale the manufacturing process from the small batches he had created to full-scale production. The company built the first of what it planned would be multiple manufacturing plants and hired a plant manager to follow the engineer's scale-up process. In the meantime, the market waited for the formal product release. The company hired a dedicated sales force to start generating interest in the product. The development engineer was promoted and assigned to a different project.

Five months later, the first manufacturing plant came on line. As the first full-size batches of the product came out of processing and into packaging, problems arose. When subjected to full-sized manufacturing, the product had tiny cracks. In the small batches prepared by the development engineer, there had never been any cracks. In expanding the product batch size by a factor of 10, however, there they were—tiny cracks. At first, no one gave the cracks much thought, because they did not affect the product characteristics or performance. But then the company shipped its first order. As the delivery truck rolled down the road, the cracks propagated throughout the product. By the time the truck arrived at the customer's facility, some of the product had broken into pieces. After two years of engineering and five months of manufacturing scale-up, the company had a great product, so long as it did not have to ship the product to anyone!

In retrospect, it is easy to identify some of the mistakes this company made. We have spent hours with groups dissecting this true story to learn from—and to not repeat—the mistakes of the past. The development engineer developed the product in isolation and did not think through scale-up issues. The company did not produce any full-sized product samples until after it had built the manufacturing plant and then discovered the propagation of the cracks. It is easy to mock management for the wasted investment.

Before being too critical, however, we should consider this point: If the final product had not developed the tiny cracks that spread during shipping, the product and the process would have been a success. In fact, many times previously, the company had used a similar process and gotten good results. Using what had worked before, those involved in this project were clueless about the risks that lurked in the shadows of their process. What is now obvious to us became obvious to them only after this product failure.

The most important lesson we can draw from this story is that we, too, are brilliant but sometimes clueless. We live in an environment of increasing global competition, an increasing pace of market changes, and a need to develop solutions that are increasingly complex. In this environment, we do not have the luxury of missteps and hidden risks. There is increasing pressure to deliver complex solutions in less time and to get it "right the first time." If we don't, we can completely miss our business value goals. The good news is that we can make sure that our brilliance results in things that work. To see how, we continue our story.

## What Went Right

With the development engineer assigned to and buried by a new project, it fell to the plant manager to sort out the issues with the propagating cracks. Fortunately, the plant manager recognized that what had worked before had not worked for the new product. Before he plunged into root cause analysis on the cracking problem, he took a huge step back, all the way back to the beginning.

Under pressure to immediately solve the problem, he asked to meet with company management. At the meeting, he asked some fairly basic questions: "How important is this product to the company? Is this a product that will provide us with a competitive advantage in the marketplace?"

His rationale for asking these questions was to get a sense of the purpose of the product. If the product would generate competitive advantage, he and the company would treat the product differently than if it did not.

The plant manager got very clear answers from the management team. This was a product that fit squarely in the company's strategy. The company's claim to fame was using recycled, recovered raw materials to produce industrial products. This product was a perfect example of the company's expertise and creativity.

In that case, the plant manager asked, could he treat this product as what it was—something that would help differentiate the company in the marketplace? Recognizing, in retrospect, the problems with the initial development, the management team gave the plant manager free rein.

The plant manager started by convening the right people. The right people included design engineers, production workers, manufacturing engineers, a sales team, and, in a surprise to everyone, one of the early-adopter customers. To make sure that the team understood all that had happened and all that needed to happen, the plant manager gave a painfully honest review of the development of the product and the issues the company had encountered in moving to full-scale production. After getting the team up to speed, the plant manager asked a gut-wrenching question: "Can we fix the problems or would the company benefit more if we halted production?" This sparked a lively discussion that ranged from necessary changes to the product development process to the humiliation of now shutting down the product line.

The plant manager let this "airing" continue for some time but then refocused the discussion on his question: "Let me ask my question another way: What made this product so critical to us when we launched the initiative?" The answers again ranged from the product's revenue potential to the commitments that had been made. The plant manager then asked a more generic question: "How do we differentiate ourselves in the marketplace?" The company had developed proprietary ways to use recycled products to make new materials. This capability had propelled the company to market-leader status. An engineer asked, "Why does that matter?" The plant manager responded, "It seems to me that if we can solve the issues, this product aligns perfectly with what makes our company unique. With this product, we have once again taken a waste material and produced something of value. For that reason, it seems we should do our best to fix the problems and get this product to market. This product exemplifies what we do. If you agree, let's move onto how we can approach the product. Ignore how we have developed the product to date. As a strategic initiative, what should we do?"

The team then sorted through the specific product features that made the product different. Only one was apparent—the use of waste material to make a usable product. With that as the principal requirement of the product, the team identified design options that could either eliminate or mitigate the full-scale production issues. Would a different form factor reduce the cracking? Or was changing the manufacturing process the only option? As the team discussed these alternatives, they associated complexity and uncertainty with each alternative. In terms of uncertainty, was there a specific market need that their product could meet? With what certainty did they understand these needs? Which form factor would the market accept, and did they know which forms were acceptable? How much did they know about the reactions taking place in the manufacturing process? How well could they link cause and effect? In terms of complexity, which options did they have to simplify the process? How could they simplify the product?

After the team mapped out the options and associated information, the plant manager asked the team which decisions they needed to make now, which decisions they could delay, and what they needed to know prior to making the decisions. All of this information was combined to provide a logical, rational approach for making the product go/kill decision and, if possible, fixing the product problems.

For example, the team could delay the go/kill decision until after the members had determined whether there was a form factor the market was dying to have. Likewise, the team could delay research into the cause of the large-batch cracking if the market would accept form factors that could be made with small batch sizes. To explore these issues further, the team members signed up for the assignments that best matched their interests and capabilities.

Over the next few weeks, the team worked through the assignments and options. Based on the work of the sales team and the early-adopter customer, the team revised the form factor. The new form factor actually met a previously unknown—at least to the company—market need. Revising the form factor enabled the company to manufacture the product in the small batch sizes it could produce without cracks. Taking this approach let the company retain most of its current investment in the manufacturing plant; it just needed to redesign its consumable molds. The team members took a more measured approach by eliminating uncertainty and complexity at each step of the process. They solved the problems they could when they could and postponed work on the most uncertain and complex issues.

Because the product was not "right the first time," the expected revenue was delayed. Also, because of the initial problems, the revenue stream grew more slowly than projected. Nevertheless, the company learned the value of the foundation tools of agile leadership.

## Why Do We Do This to Ourselves?

We were all sitting around one afternoon talking about this story. Each of us found ourselves identifying a different aspect of the story that we thought was the cause of all the travails of the organization.

We identified the initial failure of the organization to properly align its approach to the project with its true strategic nature.

We also determined that, initially, the organization did not properly lead collaboration; in fact, it did not initially have any collaboration on this particular project.

We found that the organization chose the wrong approach for the project, tackling a very complex project filled with uncertainty with a process more suited for a low-complexity and low-uncertainty project. It also assigned a leader who did not recognize the uncertainties and the complexities.

We realized that the organization did not gather all of the information it needed to make proper decisions about how to market the product and in which markets to sell the product. We also identified several cases where the company made commitments earlier than it needed to, especially with potential customers and industry partners.

As we talked about this case more, we realized that there was no *one* cause for the project's initial problems, but rather several contributing factors. When we discussed the various tools we would have used to help the company, we realized that while each tool was powerful in its own right, when put together the entire toolset could really help an organization succeed.

## A Framework of Effective Tools

What are the tools we would use to address the situation described earlier in this chapter? Through our experiences and sharing stories, we found that a collection of tools apply to how organizations approach their work, especially work that involves change and innovation; when used in moderation and in conjunction with each other, these tools can have a dramatic impact on the success of the organization. We drew the "napkin drawing" shown in Figure 1.1 to capture our thoughts, and we chose to organize this book around four main applications of those tools.

### Purpose

The Purpose Alignment Model, described in Chapter 2, generates immediately usable decision filters that leaders and teams can use to improve design. This tool evaluates business activities and options in terms of their capability to differentiate an organization's products and services in the marketplace and their mission criticality. This tool helps teams identify areas to focus their creativity and those activities and features for which "good enough" is good enough. This approach lowers direct and opportunity costs and accelerates market leadership. This simple, yet powerful, concept recognizes that not all activities should be treated in the same way. Some activities will help the organization win in the marketplace; others will help keep it in the game. We risk under- and over-investing in activities if we treat all of them as if they were identical.

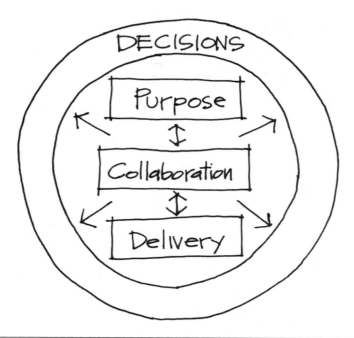

**FIGURE 1.1**    Leadership tools for use in today's complex marketplace

Here are the big ideas of Chapter 2:

- Aligning on process purpose is a smart, simple way to improve decision making.
- Designing our work around process purpose helps us quickly identify how to achieve optimal business value.
- Strategic decision filters can be cascaded throughout the organization to dramatically improve organizational alignment.

## Collaboration

As the proverb states, "No one of us is as smart as all of us." The proper use of the tools described in this book is dependent on a culture of collaboration. In the story presented earlier in this chapter, when a single person developed a product, it took more than two years to produce something that did not work. When a leader considered purpose, business value, uncertainty, and complexity in a culture of collaboration, the team made better decisions and started to generate results. Developing collaboration skills and capabilities is essential in today's dynamic marketplace. Sustainable innovation comes through collaboration. Sustainable innovation is a prerequisite to change from market follower to market leader. Today, it hinges on collaboration.

Here are the big ideas of Chapter 3:

- To develop a sustainable competitive advantage, unleash the talent in your organization to deliver innovative ideas to the marketplace and to improve the throughput and productivity in your organizations.
- The answers are in your organization.

## Delivery

Delivery is the ultimate measure of success. Any experienced leader knows that all projects are not created equal and no single approach is applicable to every project. The tool described in Chapter 4 provides a practical model for evaluating uncertainty and complexity as well as guidance for tailoring an appropriate leadership approach. The characterization of uncertainty and complexity also correlates to project risk, and we provide a roadmap for potentially reducing risk. For example, it is possible to break projects that are both highly complex and uncertain into components with lower uncertainty and risk. This process reduces the overall project risk. An understanding of complexity and risk also allows leadership to match the skills of project leaders to the needs of the project.

Here are the big ideas of Chapter 4:

- By understanding the uncertainty and complexity characteristics of your projects, you can identify better ways to lead those projects.
- High complexity or uncertainty correlates to higher risk. Reduce these factors, and you reduce your level of risk. Project decomposition can reduce complexity, while incremental delivery helps lead a project through uncertainty.
- Some leaders are natural managers of complexity, while others are experts at uncertainty. Match leadership styles to project characteristics, and develop leaders' skills to broaden their capabilities.

## Decisions

The tools we describe in this book will help you to make the key decisions you face on a regular basis, but we felt it important to discuss the actual approach to decision making. Knowing when to make your decisions and which information you need to make those decisions is very important. Chapter 5 introduces the value model tool, which provides a structure for organizing information—such as purpose, considerations, costs, and benefits—that you can use to aid your decision making.

Here are the big ideas of Chapter 5:

■ Business decisions focus on delivering value to the organization and to the marketplace. Life is much better if everyone in the organization understands what generates value and makes decisions that improve value.

■ You can develop a value model that helps you make better decisions, but this model is not just a calculation that generates a numerical value. Instead, it is a conversation that you should revisit often, especially when conditions change.

## The Leadership Tipping Point

While we describe each tool on its own and provide plenty of examples of when those tools are useful, we knew this treatment would not be complete without describing how you can put our tools to work as a leader, addressing the issues of how and when to step back and how and when to step up without rescuing your teams. This is the big idea of Chapter 6, which we call the leadership "tipping point."

Leaders can stifle progress when they interfere with team processes. At the same time, as a leader, you don't want to go over the cliff and deliver the wrong results. Sometimes leaders should stand back and let the team work—and sometimes leaders should step up and lead. In Chapter 6, we discuss how you can decide which situation you face.

## Summary

This chapter introduced the issues involved in involving the right players in your organization to gain a competitive advantage. It also introduced the framework of concepts and tools for doing so.

# CHAPTER 2

# PURPOSE

## The Big Ideas

- Aligning on process purpose is a smart, simple way to improve decision making.
- Designing our work around process purpose helps us quickly identify how to achieve optimal business value.
- Strategic decision filters can be cascaded throughout the organization to dramatically improve organizational alignment.

## An IT Project Death March

Do you remember the first time you had that sinking feeling? When you realized that, in spite of your best plans and intentions, the IT project you were leading was never going to generate enough value to justify itself? For me, the sinking feeling that triggered my soul-searching occurred at the halfway point of a 14-month, $27 million enterprise resource planning (ERP) project.

We had run the project by the book—at least as the book was then written. We had solid sponsor support, I had been able to pick the best people from the company to be on the project team, we had spent our time assessing business processes and matching them to system functionality, and we had involved a broad range of functions and levels not only in the project planning but also in the project mechanics. Even so, seven months after our official project kick-off, I knew we were in trouble. We were on budget. We were on schedule. But we were not spending our money and time on the high-impact business benefits. Instead, the bulk of our work was focused on ensuring that the new ERP system looked and acted like the legacy system we were replacing. It was becoming clear to me that we would not generate the expected business value with our project.

I did not share my concerns with my project team. Instead, I arranged a meeting with the project sponsor (the company CEO) and explained to him that while we were following our plan, I no longer believed the project would be worth the costs. He asked pointed questions about evidence that supported my concerns. Were we on budget? Yes. Were we on schedule? Yes. Then what was the problem? I had nothing concrete—just that sinking feeling. He told me to keep at it. The project was an essential foundation for the continued growth of the company. The homegrown legacy system was groaning and straining under the transactional load caused by our success. I went back to my office, but the nagging feeling of looming failure would not go away.

To the irritation of the CEO, I brought up the same concern every time I met with him to review the project. Unfortunately, I was never able to explain what was going wrong with an on-time, on-budget ERP system implementation. Only months after the "go-live" date did it become obvious to me what we had done poorly.

While the ERP project was named and treated like a strategic project, we had not aligned our numerous project decisions with the strategy of the company. In making the hundreds, if not thousands, of decisions about business processes, software functionality, and business rules, we lacked any type of strategic guidance or framework. In short, we had spent our resources on functionality that would not create sustainable competitive advantage. We had spent our time, money, and resources investing in very-low-value, or no-value functions, features, business rules, and benefits. We did not use the project to improve the business, only to replicate what we already had. We were not getting the operational and financial benefits we expected when we initially planned and justified the project. Even more sobering, we would likely never generate the expected benefits.

For example, our project planning anticipated significant improvements in inventory management. With a real-time system in place for tracking demand, on-hand inventories, and supplier lead times and tools for material planning, we expected to significantly increase our inventory turnaround time, thereby reducing our inventory costs and obsolescence. After we worked through the post "go-live" configuration and use issues, we saw some improvement, but not of the magnitude that we had expected. We still over-produced inventory, which we later wrote down, prior to writing it off entirely. We still ran out of products that our customers wanted. We still relied heavily on forecasts to predict the unpredictable future buying behavior of our customers.

We saw similar results almost across the board for each type of improvement we hoped to achieve. As another example, the legacy call center/order entry application used the following sequence of data input:

1. Customer name
2. Customer telephone number
3. Customer address

The out-of-the-box, ready-to-go sequence in the new ERP system was not exactly revolutionary:

1. Customer name
2. Customer address
3. Customer telephone number

Despite the minor difference, the call center manager was adamant that we customize the ERP system so that the new sequence of data entry was identical to that used in the legacy system (name, then telephone number, then address). So we customized the new system. We spent time, money, and resources making this customization.

Did the time and money we spent on this customization generate business value? I cannot imagine a scenario in which our customers would even notice or realize that we asked them for their address before we asked them for their telephone number. Can you imagine the company's billboards and other advertising proudly proclaiming, "Buy from us! We ask for your telephone number second!" We could have used the time and money we spent on order entry customization to do something that actually improved our business (such as better profiling our customers and matching product development to their needs)—but we didn't.

This ERP project also replaced the legacy employee expense reimbursement system. Looking back, we could have used the standard payables system to reimburse our employees for their travel and other expenses. Instead, because we were all familiar with the existing process for reimbursing our employees and had created a fairly complex set of business rules for employee reimbursement, we built a unique employee reimbursement system (which was eerily similar to the legacy employee reimbursement system), which we then integrated into the ERP system.

Did this investment generate a real benefit to the business? No. Did it allow us to make more money? Not a single cent. Did a unique employee reimbursement generate additional market share or allow us to enter new markets? Nope. Would we have gained market share with billboards that proudly proclaimed, "You will know how good we are once you see how we reimburse our employees!" Of course not. Again, I cannot imagine a scenario that makes these outcomes possible. Instead, our effort consumed resources that could have been spent on processes and activities that generated sustainable competitive advantage.

Rather than being lauded for a project that lifted the company to the next level, my team was ridiculed. We spent all this money and got what? The team must have done something wrong. Months after the project ended, I joked with my project team that we would have generated more financial value for the company if we had invested the $27 million in a money market account and collected interest during the 14-month project timeline.

## Aligning on Purpose

How could this happen? How could such an important project become almost meaningless in terms of improving company performance? Instead of generating business value, the project became a death march for both the project team and the company.

Research and personal experience indicate that this situation is all too common. IT projects start with the best of intentions. New projects are designed to capture market share, grow revenues, win customers, reduce costs, improve customer service, improve decision making, et cetera. Instead, IT projects consistently underperform. Theirs is a history of missed targets, cost overruns, extended timelines, and disappointed customers and sponsors.

We ask again: How can this happen? How can otherwise bright, intelligent, and capable project teams and organizations end up failing to deliver business value?

There is a proven way to change these results. By aligning your projects and their design based on "purpose," you improve the likelihood that you will properly allocate your time, resources, and creativity. Using purpose is a simple, yet highly effective way to change the focus of IT projects. Purpose focuses appropriate attention on what you need to win in the marketplace and what you need to avoid falling behind the market. Even better, purpose is easy to understand and easy to implement. You convert purpose from something abstract to something usable with the Purpose Alignment Model.

The Purpose Alignment Model assesses business processes or activities in two dimensions (see Figure 2.1). The first dimension is the extent to which the business activity differentiates your organization in the marketplace. The second dimension is the extent to which the business activity is critical to your mission, to your being in business.

As shown in Figure 2.1, looking at our business processes in these two dimensions yields four categories of business activities:

- Market differentiating and mission critical (we call these differentiating activities).
- Mission critical but not market differentiating (we call these parity activities).
- Market differentiating but not mission critical (we call these partnering activities).
- Neither market differentiating nor mission critical (we call these who cares activities).

We call this matrix the Purpose Alignment Model because you can use it to link these categories to their purpose. As you align how you treat these processes with their purpose, you improve your decision making and significantly improve your project and business results.

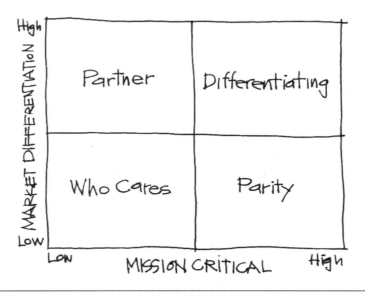

**FIGURE 2.1** The Purpose Alignment Model

Let's explain each of these categories, starting with the differentiating activities.

## Differentiating

The purpose of the differentiating activities is to excel. Because you use these activities to gain market share and to create and maintain a sustainable competitive advantage in the marketplace, you want to perform these activities better than anyone else. For your organization, these activities are or should be its claim to fame. These activities link directly to your strategy. You should be careful to not under-invest in these activities, as that would weaken your market position. In fact, you should focus your creativity on these processes. What are the differentiating activities for your organization? It depends. It depends on the specific things you do to create sustainable competitive advantage.

## Parity

The purpose of the parity activities is to achieve and maintain parity with the marketplace. Stated differently, your organization does not generate any competitive advantage if it performs these activities better than its competitors. However, because these activities are *mission critical*, you must ensure that you do not under-invest in or perform these activities poorly. Because the purpose of these activities is to be at parity in the marketplace, it also makes sense if you perform these activities in a "best practices" way. These processes are ideal candidates for simplification and streamlining, because complexity in these processes implies that you are likely over-investing. While there might be value in performing the differentiating activities in a unique way, performing the parity activities in a unique way will not generate value and could actually decrease the organization's value if your over-investment in parity processes limits the resources you can apply to differentiating processes.

For most organizations, a typical parity process is billing. Billing is clearly mission critical. If you do billing poorly, it will hurt the business. Not collecting cash or collecting cash late affects both cash flow and financial performance. Not being able to correctly invoice customers or apply payments can motivate customers to take their business elsewhere. Of course, it is equally true that you will not grow market share or gain new customers if your billing process is superior. The same goes for employee reimbursements. While this is a mission-critical activity, you typically do not equip your sales people with presentations touting the merits of your employee reimbursement process when you send them out to ring up sales. Nor should you allocate portions of your advertising budgets—what you want on your billboard—or marketing campaigns to extol your excellence in employee reimbursements.

## Partner

Some activities are not mission critical (for your organization) but can nevertheless differentiate the organization in the marketplace. The way to exploit these activities—and turn them into differentiating activities—is to find a partner with which you can combine efforts to create this differentiation. For example, a publisher might identify content development as one of its differentiating activities. This realm could include author relationships, product development, and market analysis, among other things. As its market moves more into electronic downloads of content, the publisher might recognize a market-differentiating opportunity in providing for electronic distribution of its content. However, this publisher might not have or want to develop, as a mission-critical activity, the electronic distribution of its content. In that case, the publisher might find a partner that excels at electronic distribution. This partner should know the ins and outs of the technology, and should fully understand and support digital rights management, micro-royalty calculations, and other key aspects of the electronic distribution process. Such a partnership allows the publisher to exploit electronic distribution without having to also support a set of new, mission-critical activities.

## Who Cares

Finally, some business activities are neither mission critical nor market differentiating. The goal for these activities is to perform them as little as possible. We refer to these activities as the "who cares" processes. Because these activities are neither market differentiating nor mission critical, you should spend as little time and attention as possible on them. For example, deciding the best way to provide after-hours cleaning of your offices does not deserve a complex evaluation process. Who really cares?

## Purpose Alignment Applied

Let us now apply, in retrospect, the Purpose Alignment Model to the ERP story that started this chapter. The project team spent time, money, and people customizing the software to make the sequence of data entry into the order management system match the sequence in the legacy system. While we are not sure what differentiated this company in the marketplace, we can be confident that the sequence of data entry into the order management system would not result in additional sales, customers, or market share. At best, the sequence of data entry is a parity activity; thus the time, money, and people spent customizing the order management system was an over-investment. The purpose of parity activities is to be at parity in the marketplace. The time, money, and people spent on this aspect of the ERP project were wasted. These investments increased the costs of the project without generating any business value. But that is not all: The time, money, and people devoted to the parity activity were not available to work on the high-value project benefits. Because of this and similar project decisions, the expected return was squeezed and the project turned into a death march.

# Usable Strategy and the Purpose Alignment Model

The key to using the Purpose Alignment Model is to determine what qualifies as a differentiating activity. Differentiating activities have the following characteristics:

- The specific things you do to win customers
- The specific things you do to gain market share
- The specific things you do to generate sustainable competitive advantage

This last characteristic is a big idea that links the Purpose Alignment Model to strategy.

Ideally, you will identify some simple decision criteria or filters that you can use to define what is differentiating. You can then disperse these decision filters throughout the organization so that everyone can use them, thereby ensuring that the hundreds and thousands of decisions that your employees make are aligned with purpose and strategy.

As an example, we were once asked to help a company improve its project planning and portfolio management process. The leadership of this company had spent months working through the traditional strategic planning model: agree on mission, vision, and values; then use SWOT (strengths/weaknesses/opportunities/threats) or some other method to define strategy; then use strategy to articulate long- and short-range goals; and so on. The management team had burned through several long executive retreat sessions and had almost agreed to mission and values (although vision still eluded them). We met with the executive team and told them that to make better project and portfolio decisions we needed to define some simple decision filters. We then introduced the Purpose Alignment Model. Over the course of a single collaborative session, the leadership team identified how it differentiated itself in the market place. By default, this discussion also identified the organization's strategy. Because strategy is synonymous with sustainable competitive advantage, the organization's differentiating activities were the things that created sustainable competitive advantage. In other words, its differentiating activities directly supported its strategy. We were able to distill this strategy into a usable decision filter. In this case, the company differentiated itself with a document management technology that allowed remote teams to quickly and collaboratively review and finalize legal and financial documents.

Based on this understanding, the leadership team's usable, strategically aligned decision filter became clear: "If we do this, will remote teams be able to finalize better documents faster?" This was a filter they could disseminate throughout the entire organization to improve decision making. When a project manager was presented with the option for a new feature or function that improved the project tracking module of the document management system, the project manager could ask, "Will this feature allow remote teams to finalize better documents faster?" If the answer was "No," the project manager knew that the feature was likely a parity activity, rather than a differentiating feature, and could treat it accordingly by not over-investing in the feature. For these parity features, good enough was good enough. When the CEO considered an acquisition, he could ask, "Will this acquisition allow remote teams to finalize better documents faster?" If the answer was "Yes," the CEO knew to treat the acquisition as something that would differentiate the company. If the answer was "No," the acquisition should be designed for what it did—add parity capability to the company.

This discussion is not meant to imply that traditional strategy planning does not have its place. For any organization, it is important to define mission, vision, and values. However, we rarely use mission, vision, and values to make decisions (either strategic or tactical). After all, when was the last time your portfolio management process asked, "How well does this project align with our mission?" Because the Purpose Alignment Model quickly identifies how the company generates sustainable competitive advantage, it is a nice shortcut to strategy, by using strategy as a decision filter.

## Validating the Decision Filters

Because the decision filters that you use to identify your differentiating activities are so important, it is worth validating them against their strategic intent. In their book *The Discipline of Market Leaders*, Treacy and Wiersema identified three general categories of what we call "strategic intent." Figure 2.2 shows our version of what Treacy and Wiersema describe.

If you are in the broad market, your strategy can be either product leadership or cost leadership. If you are in a niche market, you want to learn about your customers' issues so that you can be a best customer solution leader, where that best solution might range from product leadership to cost leadership, and everything in between. You can use strategic intent to ensure that your strategy—also known as sustainable competitive advantage—and your decision criteria match your target markets and needs. For example, if your strategic intent is product leadership, then your strategy might be superior consumer products. As a consequence, your differentiating decision criteria might look for ways to improve your new product development processes. If your strategic intent is the best solution for your markets' needs for customized, precision-engineered valves, then your decision criteria would seek to improve your design and engineering processes (and be content with parity in supply chain management).

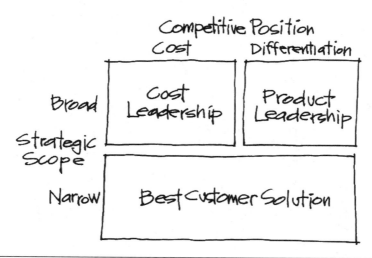

**FIGURE 2.2**   Strategic intent

## Defining What Is Differentiating

It is sometimes difficult to identify the differentiating activities. Here are some examples of what to look for. These examples also show the linkage among purpose, strategy, and strategic intent.

Suppose a large retailer has mastered its supply chain management. From its practices, what can you infer about its differentiating activities and decision filters? It is probably not a big stretch to say that this retailer's differentiating activities are its supply chain management processes. What would be the associated decision filters? How can you express them in an actionable way? How about something like, "Will this activity help optimize our supply chain as a way to sell quality products at the lowest possible price?" Suppose this is correct. How, then, might this retailer handle the technology of radio frequency identification (RFID)? Let's pass it through the filter. Will RFID help the retailer optimize its supply chain and reduce costs and prices? Suppose actual sales on a certain item are starting to fall below projections.

With RFID, the retailer can identify the inventory it has on hand and, more importantly, the inventory it has in transit, even in transit from the supplier. Armed with this knowledge, the retailer can not only adjust its orders for the items, but also intercept and redirect shipments. This practice will reduce the costs of receiving and then returning the in-transit inventory. Based on this understanding, this retailer would treat RFID as differentiating and would be an active participant in the development and implementation of RFID (because it needs RFID to maintain its sustainable competitive advantage).

Before we leave this example, let's use strategy and strategic intent to validate our decision filters. This retailer seems to have a long history of supply chain optimization. It has developed extensive supply chain and inventory optimization analytics and created innovative processes for improving material logistics. Given this history, we can guess that its strategy is supply chain optimization and its strategic intent is cost leadership. Thus the decision filters we have inferred seem to fit well with strategy and strategic intent.

Now let's consider another retailer, which has a completely different approach to the market. This retailer sells items that are priced at $1 or less. With this business model, what might be its differentiating processes? This organization needs to find products the market wants, products the retailer can sell for a dollar, and products that generate sufficient margins. Let's take a guess at a differentiating process of product selection.

This company needs a superior process to find the products that meet the previously identified criteria. How can we articulate this differentiating process as a strategic decision filter? This filter might be, "Will this activity help us select items that generate profits at a $1 sales price?" If the answer is yes, the company should treat the choice as differentiating. If not, it should treat the choice as something else.

How would this retailer approach supply chain management? If it stays true to its strategy, the company would treat supply chain management as a parity activity and mimic the best practices developed by the first retailer. Rather than developing or piloting RFID, this retailer would wait until RFID is well defined and standardized and can be implemented in a parity fashion.

Just as we did with the first retailer, let's validate our decision filters and differentiating processes with strategic intent and strategy. This retailer operates with a strategic intent of low-cost leadership; its strategy for achieving low-cost leadership is to sell products that don't cost much. As a company, this retailer seems aligned.

Next, let's compare these two retailers with a third. The third retailer is in the specialty market of outdoor sports (such as mountain biking, kayaking, and mountain climbing). The founder of this retailer is a committed outdoor enthusiast who lives what her stores sell. For this specialty retailer, what might be its differentiating activities? Supply chain optimization? Not likely. Product selection? Possibly, but with different selection criteria from the second retailer. What else?

Because this retailer targets a fairly narrow market—people who like outdoor exercise activities—its differentiating activities might be its customer analytics and intelligence. This retailer needs to match the needs of its customers—often before its customers know they have a need—with its product selection processes. Thus we can guess at decision filters that seek to discover the next great outdoor exercise trend. The retailer's strategy is to be the market maker in outdoor products. In terms of strategy and strategic intent, it is a best customer solution company, with a strategy of helping its customers take their outdoor exercise to the next level. In practice, this company is a leader in customer segmentation and has a finely honed process for finding fairly obscure products that it can explode into the outdoor exercise market.

As you would expect, this retailer treats supply chain optimization as a parity activity. The same is true of most of its operational processes. While the first two retailers don't pay much attention to store layout and product display, this outdoor sports retailer uses layout and displays to match its customer segmentation.

A manufacturer of industrial equipment promotes its products' lower lifetime cost of ownership. In its market, it created the "lifetime cost of ownership" metric. What are its differentiating processes? The engineering activities that lead to improved fuel economy, ease of maintenance, and ease of operations. Its decision filter is simply, "Will this activity help us reduce the lifetime cost of our equipment?" As a result, the organization has created technology to improve fuel injection and lengthen the time between maintenance cycles. Because this company operates in a niche market (after all, how broad is the market for industrial equipment?), it is a best customer solution company, but its best customer solution is to be the leader in lowest lifetime cost. Its primary competitor competes as the low-price leader and focuses its innovation on ways to reduce the initial sales price of its equipment.

As a final example, suppose a fast-food chain has a very simple menu. Reminiscent of Henry Ford's famous dictum, you can have any hamburger you like, as long as you like it plain. Another chain constantly introduces new menu items, including short-term special menus. We can imagine the decision filters for the first chain: "Will this activity allow us to maintain a simple, easy-to-understand and easy-to-order-from menu?" With this question being what defines differentiating, we would expect that this chain's test kitchen is a pretty boring place to work. Not so for the second chain, as its managers regularly hold internal contests to identify the next big fast-food hit.

For each of these companies, the Purpose Alignment Model provides an immediately usable framework for improving decision making. The decision filters that help each company define differentiating activities also articulate strategy. And not a nebulous, ethereal strategy, either—rather, a strategy that everyone in the organization can use to make the multitude of decisions that occur each day, a strategy that defines its sustainable competitive advantage. Will this decision help you put more variety in your menu? If so, you need to do this activity better than your competitors. If not, you should make the decision in a parity fashion. Will the functionality of your customer loyalty program help you create a menu with more variety? It just might if you can use your loyalty program to gather menu ideas and measure the effectiveness of your previous menu items. Will the functionality of your inventory management system help you create menu variety? Probably not, so you should design your inventory management system based on best, simple practices. The same goes for the design of your chart of accounts—and for a whole host of other decisions. Knowing which strategic decision filter the company uses, a purchasing agent can self-filter decisions and requests. So can a product manager. So can the chief financial officer and the chief information officer.

If defining strategy is still a challenge, there are two tools that can help. First, you can use the traditional strengths, weaknesses, opportunities, and threats (SWOT) analysis method. Using SWOT, you collaborate to determine—no surprise here—your organizational and market strengths, weaknesses, opportunities, and threats. As you discuss and sort through the SWOT results, you can begin to infer and then articulate your sustainable competitive advantage (also known as strategy).

A very usable alternative to SWOT analysis is the Five Questions:

- Who do we serve and what do they want and need most?
- What do we provide to help them?
- What is the best way to provide this?
- How do we know we are succeeding?
- How should we organize to deliver?

The Five Questions go beyond typical strategy to include distribution methods, measures, and organizational design.

We have found the Five Questions very useful if a leadership team or project team is having a hard time identifying what is differentiating. The answer to the first question helps define the organization's target market and its various needs. The answer to the second question helps you define the specific things your company does to meet these needs. These are the same things you are or should be doing to differentiate your firm in the marketplace. That is, you should be doing them as long as there is a market need for what you think differentiates your organization in the marketplace. The answers to the rest of the questions help you sort through your business model options, performance measures, and organizational design.

To summarize the process used to implement the Purpose Alignment model, you first use the model to identify the differentiating activities and decision filters. These also yield your proposed strategy (also known as sustainable competitive advantage). You then validate the proposed strategy using strategic intent, SWOT analysis, and the Five Questions. This approach gives you everything you need to improve decision making and resource allocation—valid, immediately usable decision filters that you can disseminate throughout the organization.

## Purpose at the Project Level

The Purpose Alignment Model works as well at the project level as it does at the organizational level. Project teams can collaboratively define the decision filters and determine which, if any, of the features and functions in their project fall into the differentiating, parity, partnering, or who cares categories. Even if the organization has not defined strategy, we have yet to encounter a project team that cannot correctly and adequately define strategically aligned, usable decision filters. The following examples illustrate how project teams have used the Purpose Alignment Model to dramatically improve the typical project results.

A project team was tasked with upgrading the company's pricing engine. The existing business rules for product pricing included dimensions for the following items:

- Product family
- Product category
- Product
- Per-order quantity
- Historical customer purchase volume
- Customer credit history

The price to be charged a specific customer was a combination of these six dimensions. As you might expect, this required a fairly complex pricing system. Because these pricing dimensions had grown over time, the pricing engine was never really architected and so was difficult to use. In fact, the pricing business rules and engine were so complex that a full-time person was required to administer changes in the products, categories, and structure seasonal and sales programs. The pricing engine was also complex enough that it was getting in the way of the chief marketing officer's (CMO) plans. This complexity discouraged changes to the product and discount structure. Eventually, the CMO requested an overhaul of the pricing engine.

The chief information officer (CIO) assigned a team to work on the requirements. The project manager felt that this venture was an ideal project for the Purpose Alignment Model. The project manager introduced the model to the team and asked, "What differentiates us in the marketplace—the products we develop and produce or our product pricing schemes?"

It took the team a few seconds to agree that the products were differentiating and that pricing was a parity concern (although the project manager did have to fight back a few frustrated team members who felt that pricing was a who cares business process). As a parity process, pricing was an ideal candidate for best practices and simplification. This approach would avoid not only an over-investment in a parity activity, but also the future problems that accompany the complexity, such as system upgrades. That was the easy part. Now the project manager had to have the same conversation with the project sponsor, the CMO.

Not wanting to face the CMO by himself, the project manager asked which team members wanted to attend the meeting with him. To his surprise, they all signed up for the meeting. The project manager arranged the meeting with the CMO and took nearly the same approach as with the project team. He started by stating, "We need your help. We need some type of guidelines we can use as we sort through our design options for the pricing engine project. As a team, we have started using a fairly simple model that seems to help us. Can we work through this model with you?"

Who could say no?

"This model measures business rules in two dimensions. First, do we use the rules to gain market share? Second, are the business rules mission critical for us? In other words, do we need to have these business rules, like our purchasing and payables process, just to be a reliable, quality company? Using these two dimensions, we can draw the following quadrant."

The project manager then drew the Purpose Alignment Model.

"Clearly, we want our top-right business rules to be superior. The bottom-right rules should be at parity with our competition. We want to use this model for the pricing engine project but need your help. As we think through how we differentiate ourselves in the market, we think that our products fall into this differentiating category. Do you agree?"

The CMO agreed.

"If it is our products that differentiate us, where do our pricing business rules belong? It seems to us that pricing rules are not the reason people do business with us. We certainly can't have really strange or subpar pricing rules. This causes us to think that pricing rules are a parity process, and not a differentiating factor. Do you agree?"

The CMO paused longer before answering.

"I do think our pricing rules are important. It sounds as if you are discounting them completely."

"We agree that they are important. In fact, they are mission critical. We just don't think we use our pricing rules to gain market share. We have to do pricing really well, but not better than anyone else."

The CMO thought some more.

"Okay. I can see what you are saying. If I agree, what does that mean for my project?"

"What it means is that we don't want to over-invest in the system to support a parity process—pricing. Instead, we want to work with you on a pricing model that is based on best industry practices and is simple. We think our design goal should be an understandable—even by our customers—pricing model that is easy to administer. This would allow us to adapt to market conditions more easily. You know how difficult we now find it to do seasonal and special pricing? If we treat pricing as a parity process, we can improve our flexibility by reducing the complexity. If pricing is a parity process, our design goal for this project is different than if pricing is a differentiating process."

The CMO bought into this approach and assigned the team to explore simple best pricing practices. The new pricing engine was based on standardized product pricing. Each product had its standard price; actual customer pricing was then based on discounts off the standard price. The discounts were based on each customer's previous year's sales volumes. If customers had purchased more the previous year, they got higher discounts this year. This pricing model, which was simple both to implement and to communicate, enabled the company to apply seasonal or special discounts and encouraged customers to purchase more from the company as a way to qualify for higher future discounts. While pricing rules were not what differentiated the company, it turned out that its complex pricing model was actually under parity. Most customers embraced the new, simpler pricing model. The old model was so confusing that they often could not sort out why there were paying certain prices for the company's products.

A different company used the Purpose Alignment Model to ensure that its software product was a marked improvement over the existing technology. This company developed software for the creation of financial documents. The document creation projects the software supported tended to include a wide range of people from different organizations. In-house and external attorneys, internal and external finance and accounting personnel, external auditors, and bankers, among others, all collaborated on these financial documents. This company's software was designed to improve the remote creation, revision, and finalization of these documents. The company had committed to and planned a major upgrade of its software. The project plan consisted of five major modules:

- Document Edit
- Project Management
- Document Management
- Documentation Templates and Library
- EDGAR Integration

The proposed work on these five modules totaled nearly 3000 story points. Before the company officially started work on the project, the chief technology officer (CTO) paused long enough to pass these five major components through the Purpose Alignment Model. The market was dominated by larger companies that enjoyed a decided advantage in project management, document management, document library, and EDGAR integration. However, the market lacked a way to effectively gather the various responses from the multitude of document reviewers and collaboratively and efficiently agree on a final version of sentences, paragraphs, and sections.

With the help of the CTO, the company managers agreed that a dramatic improvement in document editing capabilities could differentiate their product in the marketplace. It made perfect sense for this company's billboard to read, "We provide a superior way to collaborate on and improve financial documents." The managers also agreed that the other modules were parity issues for their company and did not need to be superior to the existing technology. The company then focused its creativity on ways to improve its online document edit vision and technology. This effort resulted in slightly more than 300 story points of development that set a new standard for document collaboration, revision, and editing. By agreeing that the other modules needed to be "good enough," the company also significantly reduced the costs of developing the other story points. The net result was a product that, rather than being a "me too," represented a quantum-leap improvement, yet reduced the cost and timeline of the development project by more than 40%.

As another example, as part of an ERP implementation, a development team was asked to customize the ERP package to replicate the legacy accounts receivable system. The legacy system included 32 flavors of credit. As you might expect, this was a daunting assignment. The 32 types of credit had grown up with the company and so were not part of a comprehensive customer strategy. Rather, the CFO and the vice president of sales brainstormed new credit models and then asked IT to implement the models into the legacy system. The expectation for the new ERP system was that it would support these 32 credit models.

As the development team started to sort through this requirement, its members passed the credit terms through the Purpose Alignment Model. Not surprisingly, the team decided that unique and interesting credit terms were not how the company differentiated itself in the marketplace. The development team used its informal version of a decision filter to determine that credit terms were parity issues. This filter was, "If this differentiates us, it belongs on our billboards." The development team could not imagine any company billboards or advertisements that proudly proclaimed, "Buy from us! We have more credit-terms choices than anyone!" The team met with the CFO and VP of sales and explained their billboard filter. Before the CFO and the VP of sales could argue, the team explained that it felt that the credit terms were extremely important, but their importance did not come from their uniqueness or variety. Although the credit terms were mission critical, investing in the system complexity necessary to support 32 types of credit seemed an overinvestment in a parity activity. The VP of sales interrupted the team by stating that he agreed and that there needed to be only four types of credit:

- High-volume customers that paid their bills.
- High-volume customers that did not pay their bills.
- Low-volume customers that paid their bills.
- Low-volume customers that did not pay their bills. (The VP of sales later refined this category by stating that low-volume customers that did not pay their bills would not get credit; they must pay before their orders shipped.)

The Purpose Alignment Model is not the answer to everything. However, it is a highly effective, easy-to-implement tool that improves process, business rule, feature, and function designs and decisions.

## Caveats and Lessons Learned

For the sake of full disclosure, we have collected the following warnings and lessons learned about the Purpose Alignment Model.

**It is important—no, critical—to emphasize (and then emphasize again, and then stress) the mission-critical nature of the parity activities.** Culturally, we associate our self-worth and value to the organization with the process and business rules we control and use. This creates a natural tendency to want our process and business rules to be "differentiating." If you don't emphasize and communicate the mission-critical nature of the parity activities, people will resist the use of the model and its associated decision filters. Alternatively, they may attempt to contort their processes so they fall into the differentiating category. This defeats the effective use of the model.

**What is a differentiating activity changes over time.** As soon as you unleash on the market your improvements to your differentiating processes, business rules, functions, and features, the market can now mimic what you have done. Therefore, you need a focused, working innovation process that constantly updates your roadmap with new improvements to your differentiating activities.

**What is a parity activity changes over time.** Best practices for your parity activities can change. As soon as a process improvement becomes the new standard, it creates a parity gap that you need to fill. Of course, to fill the gap, you can then mimic what someone else has already invented rather than invent it yourself. Doing so requires an internal process to find and implement best practices.

**Purpose is not priority.** Purpose identifies the design goals of a process, business rule, function, or feature. It does not define the sequence in which the work on that process, rule, function, or feature must occur. That being said, purpose can provide a framework for strategic and tactical planning.

First, you apply our decision filters to segregate your processes, business rules, functions, and features into the appropriate quadrants. You then perform a gap analysis on your processes, business rules, functions, and features. This gap analysis helps you identify potential projects—namely, projects to fill the gaps.

You might identify serious gaps in your differentiating processes. If so, you can then develop a strategic plan to fill those gaps. This plan might also include some enabling parity gaps that need to be filled. For example, one company recognized that it needed dramatic improvements in its decision-making process, which led it to identify a gap in its decision support tools. However, before it could tackle the problem of decision support tools, this organization first needed to close a gap in data collection and quality. Both of these issues were parity activities. The company's decision support strategic plan was based on designing its data collection and quality processes around improved decision support.

**Analytics can be differentiating.** If you can make better decisions, particularly about your differentiating processes, you improve your ability to compete in the marketplace. Analysis that seeks to better understand your differentiating processes can also be differentiating. Not all analytics are differentiating, however. For example, a large retailer that differentiates itself through its superior supply chain management focuses its unique and differentiating analytics on the supply chain. It does not do anything special to analyze customers or product performance, but rather accepts standard analysis methods for customers and products. This approach allows the retailer to focus its creativity on all aspects—including analysis—of supply chain management.

**Treat exceptions like exceptions.** Although we are skeptical, you might be able to justify creating processes, business rules, functions, and features to handle exceptions in the differentiating quadrant. However, we cannot think of any situation that justifies customizing processes, business rules, functions, or features to handle exceptions in the parity quadrant. If there are exceptions, treat them like exceptions—in other words, do not codify or institutionalize their handling.

For example, a multichannel specialty retailer was replacing its legacy order management and credit card processing systems. At the start of the project, the team had used the Purpose Alignment Model with the executive team to define the company's decision filters and differentiating activities. This retailer competed as a best customer solution company and focused its solutions on a specific market niche—people who liked to participate in extreme outdoor sports. As a result, its differentiating activities were its product selection and management processes and customer service. The retailer had two decision filters: "Will this activity help us select products that our customers use to get an outdoor thrill?" and "Will this activity help us create a lifelong customer?" As you might expect, the order management and credit card processing business rules and systems were deemed parity activities. Their value derived from their excellence, not from their uniqueness. The team took a best practices, standardized approach to the business rules and functionality of these systems, and the project moved along quickly and without the typical customizations and complexity. A few weeks before the new systems were scheduled to go live, the call center manager approached the project team leader and declared, "We forgot about split payments!"

The project leader was quiet for a few moments and then replied, "Split what?"

"Split payments. In the old system, we allowed people to pay for their orders with multiple credit cards."

"We did? Why?"

"It is a customer service issue. When a customer calls into the call center to place an order and wants to use more than one credit card, our current order management system lets us enter the different credit cards and the credit card processing handles however many we enter."

This was the first time that the project leader had heard of split payments, and he remained skeptical: "We really do this? I hate to be redundant, but why?"

"It is for customer service. And, because one of our differentiating activities is customer service, it occurs to me that this is something we need to do in the new system. I apologize because I forgot about this issue until now. As we were testing the new system, I remembered split payments. Because they are part of a differentiating activity, don't we have to implement them?"

The project leader thought through the initial discussions about sustainable competitive advantage and the differentiating activities. "One of the things we talked about for our differentiating activities was that they were differentiating if we thought we could use the activities to gain market share. If split payments are truly differentiating, they will help us win customers. Given that, we need to advertise split payments, right? Do you think split payments belong on our billboards? Should we go into the marketplace with the message, 'You should buy from us because we can handle your combination of credit cards'?"

The call center manager thought through whether split payments actually gained market share for the company. "No, they don't differentiate us—but they are still a customer convenience. Is there something we can do?"

"Let me ask you this: How often does someone ask us to process multiple credit cards? How many times a day or week?"

"As I think about it, not that often. Perhaps three to five times per week." This was out of an average weekly volume of more than 10,000 orders.

The project leader then responded, "In that case, what we have is not a differentiating activity, but rather an exception. We should treat exceptions like exceptions. If this feature is something we want to continue to offer, we should see if we can find a way to handle split payments within the standard functionality of the new systems. If so, we do it. If not, we will have to deal with that issue outside the system. But, because split payments happen so rarely, we can do that."

The call center manager agreed. If they could be handled without the expense and complexity of a system customization, split payments were worth supporting.

The project leader and call center manager took the split payments request back to the team. The team sorted through the options and quickly developed a solution within the standard functionality of the new order management and credit card processing systems. It was not an elegant solution, and it required manual intervention from someone in the credit department to finish processing an order. Even so, handling such a transaction three to five times a week did not put an onerous burden on the credit department.

**The focus shifts to behavior change.** Using the Purpose Alignment Model is common sense—but it is not common practice. In other words, people often behave as if parity processes require uniqueness or as if differentiating processes can be also-rans. Changing this thinking and behavior is always a challenge and requires the normal change management tools. One advantage of the Purpose Alignment Model is that it is simple to explain, understand, and use. Ideally, you can distill the results of this model down to simple guidelines that people can use to revise their own behavior and thinking.

**It takes practice.** Although the Purpose Alignment Model is easy to explain and use, it takes practice to deal with the different perspectives that people have about the processes, business rules, functions, and features that they own and use. Sometimes, you will make mistakes and incorrectly classify a process. As with all learning activities, practice eventually makes perfect.

# Getting Started

We have found that the best way to implement the Purpose Alignment Model is to first define the decision criteria you use to identify your differentiating processes. Once you have identified the very small number of truly differentiating activities (you cannot excel at everything), most everything else falls into the parity category. You can then assess whether you are treating your differentiating activities in a differentiating way and your parity activities in a parity way. Each time you need to make a design choice, you can then ask yourself the question, "Is this a differentiating or parity activity?"

For example, a company had recently acquired two competing companies. Each of the now-three divisions used different payroll processing systems. The VP of human resources had decided that the company would standardize on one system and scheduled a three-day meeting with representatives from all three divisions to hammer through the decision about which of the three (or perhaps a completely new) payroll systems all divisions would use. As you might expect, each division prepared for the meeting by gathering good information about its payroll system and bad information about the other two payroll systems. The battle lines were being drawn; the defenses were being designed.

The meeting started. The VP of human resources kicked off the meeting by drawing the Purpose Alignment Model on the whiteboard, giving a short explanation, and asking, "Is payroll processing a differentiating or parity activity?" Each of the three divisions competed in different ways, but all three recognized that payroll processing was mission critical (the company had to do it right) but not market differentiating (the company did not gain market share via payroll processing).

Once all of the meeting attendees agreed that payroll processing was a parity activity, the VP of human resources took the next step: "If payroll processing is a parity activity, we should mimic best practices and find ways to streamline our payroll processing. Given this goal, what probably matters is that we select a parity payroll system—not which particular system we choose." Everyone agreed and changed their payroll system selection criteria to the system that most effectively supported best practices (and all three did) at the lowest total cost of ownership and least disruption. Within 15 minutes, all three divisions had agreed on which payroll system to use.

The rest of the three days of scheduled meetings was spent standardizing all of the payroll business rules across all three divisions. The participants standardized items down to the level of nomenclature and codes. The resulting payroll implementation was a non-event. Setting the stage with the Purpose Alignment Model created a group agreement on what the goals of the project were and how best to meet those goals.

## A Comprehensive Case Study

The telephone call came at the end of a long day: "We need to replace our legacy business system. We asked around and several people suggested we give you a call."

My reply was immediate: "A legacy system replacement? We live for legacy system replacements. However, our approach is quite different from the traditional method. Are you open to that?"

"My last big IT project was such a nightmare that I will consider anything to not have to live through that again. Sure, we are open to your approach."

I gave the caller, Mark, the CIO of Lifebrands, a multichannel consumer packaged goods (CPG) company, a quick overview of the Purpose Alignment Model and explained how we had applied it to similar, large-scale, put-the-business-at-risk projects. I also described our track record and noted that the track record of the Purpose Alignment Model was pretty good (actually, very good) at improving project and business success. This information teased Mark enough that he agreed to meet with us to discuss his project.

We met in person a few days later. Lifebrands had grown from a one-person operation managed by the founder to more than 1500 employees in a matter of 10 years. As you might expect with such rapid growth, the legacy system was a hodge-podge of technologies made up of both commercial and custom software. As Lifebrands continued to grow, it became apparent that the legacy system could not keep pace and needed to be replaced. The question was how to proceed. The founder and CEO had heard enough nightmare stories about systems implementations that he was nervous about the ability of the company to go through such a wrenching experience. Mark had joined Lifebrands the year before, and he did not want to be the person who brought the company to its knees via a systems replacement project.

Lifebrands had started down the path of a traditional system replacement project. The IT department members were gathering requirements by interviewing the various departments in the company. They would then translate these requirements into a request for proposal that they would send to various software companies. The software companies would respond with a requirements gap analysis (i.e., we perfectly support the requirement, somewhat support the requirement, or don't support the requirement, along with an explanation of how the software company would fill any gaps in its support of the requirement). Lifebrands would use this response to winnow its choices to the top three software vendors and then schedule extended product demonstrations. These demonstrations would enable a cross-functional selection team to see how well the software products fit their requirements and select the first- and second-place winners. The selection team would then figure out how to customize the software to fill in the functionality gaps. This analysis would lead the team members to their final decision. They would then start, the project assuming a combination of off-the-shelf and custom software would replace their legacy system.

During our meeting, Mark confessed that the team was nearly halfway complete with gathering the requirements and that it was this requirements gathering activity that had motivated him to find someone—us—to help him.

"As we talk with the various departments about what they need in the new system, it seems that what they want is a new system that is identical to the legacy system. The requirements we have gathered so far aren't so much requirements as they are a perfect description of the legacy system. Yet, the problems with the legacy system are well known and understood. If this project is to spend money to replicate the legacy system, we should just stick it out with the legacy system."

We took out a clean piece of paper and drew on it a quadrant.

"Let's look at your business processes and, therefore, your new system requirements, from two perspectives. First, let's consider the extent to which they differentiate you in the marketplace. Second, let's identify the extent to which they are mission critical to your operations. This yields the following four types of business processes."

We wrote in "Differentiating," "Parity," "Partnering," and "Who Cares?"

"If your organization is like most other companies, you have a few processes that are differentiating. That means the vast majority of your business processes fall into the parity category. Because the purpose of the parity processes is help your company be at parity in the marketplace, these processes should be as simple as possible (because complexity among these processes will cost you dearly in the short and long term) and based on industry best practices.

"If your organization is like most other companies, we suspect that most of the new system requirements you have gathered and will gather are for parity processes. You are frustrated because you are on the path to select and then customize a system—a very expensive proposition—just to make your parity processes unique. Do we have it right?"

Mark responded, "You have it exactly correct. This is exactly what we need to do. This changes everything. How can we start using this model?"

We spent the rest of our time that day planning how Mark could use the Purpose Alignment Model to focus the company on a project that would enhance and improve the current state, rather than just spending money to replicate the current state. Mark asked us to meet with the company founder and CEO to get his buy-in to use the model for the system replacement project.

A week later, we met with Mark and David, the founder and CEO of Lifebrands. Mark introduced the theme of the meeting by describing his unease with the current method for selecting and then implementing the new system. He explained that we had developed an approach that made much more sense than what Lifebrands had been doing and then asked us to explain our approach. We once again drew a quadrant, this time on the whiteboard in David's office. We explained the Purpose Alignment Model using the example of how a different company had used the model for its system replacement project. We also explained how the other company had used the decision filters it had defined to create new growth opportunities.

David asked several questions during our whiteboard demonstration. As we were winding down, he said, "When I started this company, I was proud of how we kept things simple. But over the past 10 years, we seem to have adopted complexity as our goal. A couple of weeks ago, someone asked me what, knowing what I know now, I would change about our company. I told him, 'I would start over and keep things simple.' I am sold on this approach. I want to use your model for our system project, but use it in a way that we can then leverage it to everything we do."

We then sorted through the logistics of how to present the model to the members of the management team. Our goal was to define the decision filters that the project team could use for the software selection and implementation decisions.

Two weeks later, we met with the management team in a working session. David had already reviewed the model with the managers, and we had sent them materials about the model in advance. The team members came to the meeting ready to sort through the options. As is usually the case, we first needed to play "bad cop" on some of the ideas about what differentiated Lifebrands. Lifebrands' legal counsel felt very strongly that the Lifebrands process for intellectual property (IP) protection differentiated the company in the marketplace. He gave several seemingly compelling arguments to advance his cause. Just when it seemed as if "IP protection" was going to land in the differentiating quadrant, we asked the VP of sales a simple question: "When was the last time you sealed a deal by touting

Lifebrands' excellence in IP protection? When was the last time you felt you should include a description of the IP protection process in sales presentations and collateral? If IP protection is differentiating, you are missing opportunities by not using it to gain market share."

The answer was obviously "Never," and we used this answer to explain our billboard filter. By now, the legal counsel had gotten into the spirit. His next suggestion was that, if IP protection was differentiating, he had some billboard design ideas. For example, how about a billboard that showed a pair of hands in handcuffs with the title, "Our IP protection is good enough to tie your hands"?

After a few more, similar suggestions, David, the CEO, piped in. "IP protection is important; in fact, it is mission critical. But it is not our core competency; it is not what makes us special. Rather than try to figure out how to make what each of us does fit into the differentiating category, we accept that what we do is important because it is mission critical. With that out of the way, let's focus on how we really do differentiate ourselves. What are your ideas?"

Over the next several minutes, we developed a consensus that Lifebrands' claim to fame was its ability to develop products with proven efficacy and distribute those products in multiple channels without creating channel conflicts. This idea formed the basis for two decision filters:

- Will this activity help us develop products with proven results?
- Will this activity help us distribute into our channels without creating conflicts?

That was it. With these two questions, Lifebrands had a fully articulated strategy. The company now knew where to focus its innovation efforts. By default, everything else was deemed a parity, partnering, or who cares activity.

We then turned our attention to the system replacement project. Which system business rules, functions, and features supported the differentiating activities? The only one we could think of was product and channel analytics. Everything else (e.g., financials, inventory, supply chain, customer relationship management, warehouse management, IP protection) was linked to parity activities. As such, rather than gathering requirements in the traditional way, Lifebrands would assume that market-leading software adequately supported these parity activities. The software selection criteria would then change. Because Lifebrands would assume that the parity functionality was supported, the criteria would now be total cost of ownership, ease of implementation, and ease of integration. There would still be software product demonstrations from the leading software providers, but the purpose of these demonstrations would be to learn and understand the gap between how Lifebrands performed the transactions and how the software performed the transactions. Because Lifebrands would adopt the best practices way the software performed the transactions, the demonstrations would help the selection team identify which Lifebrands processes needed to change and how they needed to change.

This approach, in turn, completely changed Lifebrands' schedule and budget. The project plan had assumed a significant amount of time and money would be needed to customize the new software to match the Lifebrands processes. With the new approach, these resources were no longer necessary for customization of parity processes. Instead, Lifebrands could allocate the time and money to work on the analytics that would drive improved decision making.

In the course of a two-hour meeting, Lifebrands had achieved the following results:

- Selected an immediately implementable and communicated strategy
- Adopted a less-complex, lower-risk, lower-cost project
- Identified the high-impact benefits (product and channel analytics) that would help it win in the marketplace
- Placed the appropriate emphasis on the parity activities

After this meeting, there was still plenty to do. We needed to disseminate the decision criteria throughout the organization and practice using the criteria on the system replacement project. Over the course of the next several months, Lifebrands got used to using the Purpose Alignment Model as a decision-making tool.

The effects on the system replacement project were significant. By accepting and adopting standard software functionality, Lifebrands was able to reduce its project budget by 40% and its timeline by 50%. In other words, the original project plan anticipated that 40% of the money and 50% of the time would go toward over-investing in parity functionality. Lifebrands spent a portion of this saved money and time to experiment with different methods to improve its analysis of products and channels. As it gained more visibility into the combination of product performance and channel performance, it was able to make more targeted decisions about which products to place in which channels.

This case study is not meant to imply that taking the Purpose Alignment Model approach was easy. It was not. Even so, it was a significant improvement over how Lifebrands had started the project and process. As the project wound down, David, the Lifebrands CEO, said, "Why would you ever do something like this any other way?

## Summary

Imagine the power you can unleash if everyone in your organization makes strategically and tactically aligned decisions. In such an environment, you can focus your creativity on the activities that generate sustainable competitive advantage, while you focus your efforts to achieve operational excellence in those areas where you need to be good, not great. This is the power of the Purpose Alignment Model. It is an intuitive, easy-to-understand, easy-to-implement model that you can disperse throughout the organization. As you read this chapter, you may have identified your own differentiating projects that deserve unique treatment. You likely also identified parity projects that should be simplified and streamlined. If so, you are ready to use the model to make better decisions.

# CHAPTER 3

# COLLABORATION

## The Big Ideas

- To develop a sustainable competitive advantage, unleash the talent in your organization to deliver innovative ideas to the marketplace and to improve the throughput and productivity in your organizations.
- The answers are in your organization.

## Picking Money Up Off the Floor

"Pollyanna, we're at capacity! We have projects we can't do because we can't find the people." A midlevel architecture firm couldn't find enough architects to meet their customer needs. Too many buildings to design and not enough people to design them—money on the floor and the leaders of the company couldn't pick it up. This was a real pain point for the partners.

"We have more than enough in our pipeline; we've got to increase the throughput of our projects." In the "feast or famine" architecture business, having a full pipeline that you cannot deliver on is frustrating.

"Let's ask the people in your company how to improve the project throughput" was my reply. There was silence. I could see it on their faces: I was the consultant. Didn't they hire me because I had the answers? "Let's see if your employees know what is slowing down their workflow and how they can improve their own productivity." Tentatively they agreed. After meeting with everyone in the company in small working teams, they arrived at more than 150 suggestions and action items—action items they themselves took ownership of and implemented. One year later, the company had increased its revenues by 90% while increasing its resources by only 35%. It managed to pick up most of the money it had previously been leaving on the floor. Collaboration was the key: Members of the firm worked together not only to discover the obstacles to productive projects, but also to remove them.

How responsive is your organization to the new ideas that will improve operations as well as develop breakthrough product lines and services? And how do you foster innovation and creativity in your company to increase productivity and profits? The answers your organization needs to succeed are very likely to be found within the people who work with you. Your teams on the frontlines know best how to lead change with subtle product improvements, bold new directions, and improved services that will strengthen your organization's position in the marketplace.

How do you lead the development of innovative practices and processes to improve productivity *and* stimulate the ideas you need to lead in your market? This goal is certainly not achieved alone. As the Japanese proverb says, "None of us are as smart as all of us." The answers to your company's needs are to be found within your organization; the task at hand is to unleash the talent of your people while simultaneously fostering the free flow of ideas among all the stakeholders in your enterprise. People at every level in your organization have the ability to anticipate and the power to innovate. Indeed, it is very likely that some of the best ideas will be found in unexpected places. Your sales team may have ideas about streamlining production and reducing costs, in addition to passing along new product ideas based on their interactions with customers. An engineer may blurt out the best marketing idea you've heard in a long time. Talented leaders actively seek out these kinds of responses and look for them in every area of the company. Great leaders know how to create open, collaborative environments where ideas are freely and vigorously exchanged as a regular part of day-to-day operations. They build cross-functional teams that bring diverse skills and points of view to bear on a new problem or opportunity, and they do so with efficiency and speed. Great leaders foster continual innovation in an environment where people "own" their personal and collective performance and maximize their contributions.

Successful companies employ collaboration. But the key question is this: How do leaders create and lead these collaborative organizations, companies, and teams? In this chapter we will describe three processes and the tools to go with them that will enable members of your organization to collaborate, and will enable you to lead that collaboration:

### ■ Collaboration Steps

1. Create an open environment, where ideas flow freely.
2. Convene people from all disciplines and relevant areas of the organization.

3. Discover issues and solutions using the collaboration process.
4. Stand back and let people work.

■ **Collaboration Process**
1. Agree on the goal, topic, problem, or purpose.
2. Brainstorm.
3. Group ideas.
4. Prioritize results.
5. Let people volunteer for what they will do and by when.

■ **Leading Collaboration**
1. Get the right people in your organization.
2. Trust first!
3. Let people collaborate in determining the direction of your organization.
4. Stand back.

Let's take a closer look at each set of tools.

## Collaboration: Step by Step

How do you collaborate? Stimulating and maintaining the flow of ideas within an organization is a multifaceted endeavor. To collaborate is to unleash the free flow of creative ideas in your organization—to create the next generation of products and services that will enable your company to compete and lead in the marketplace and that will streamline its operations to increase productivity and decrease costs.

1. **Create an open environment**—an environment characterized by trust; nonjudgmental, open communication; and transparency. Without these elements, the natural creativity of your team will never emerge. Instead, doubt, uncertainty, and fear will keep people from speaking up when a problem is identified, ideas are discovered, or a solution is found.
2. **Assemble the right team of people.** Assign the best minds in your organization to the task of generating ideas and set the goals using a strategic framework of collaboration.

3. **Stimulate the flow of ideas using a collaboration process.**
   Encourage and capture creative solutions with participation
   from all areas of responsibility, where individual team members
   decide what needs to happen and provide time frames to deliver
   results.

4. **Stand back and let people work.** Support the process in every
   way you can.

The next sections of this chapter look at each of these steps and the
tools you will need in detail.

## Step 1: Create an Open Environment

What is an open environment? What kind of organization stimulates a
free flow of ideas, encourages open questioning in discussions, and values all inputs? It takes a great deal of confidence for a leader, and for a
corporate culture, to truly value openness. When an organization is
plagued by insecurity, fear, and a need to exert high levels of control,
the environment itself undermines the kind of flexibility required for
collaboration.

An open environment does the following:

- Stimulates creativity and innovation
- Fosters the emergence of methods that lead change and that
  respond quickly to changing markets
- Supports open communication between different cultures after
  mergers and acquisitions
- Provides just-in-time development and adjustments in operations
  and processes to deliver results and achieve corporate goals

Participants in collaboration seminars have identified and prioritized
the characteristics of an open environment. According to these sources,
the top characteristics are trust and integrity, transparency, fearlessness,
communication, and autonomy.

### Trust and a Culture of Trust

Trust is essential to productive teams. Without trust, team members can
waste time in clarifying communication and protecting their own backs.
Unfortunately, you can't *make* people trust one another.

As the leader, your role, style, and behavior will lay the groundwork for building trust. There are a few things about *yourself* that you need to pay special attention to. Authenticity is essential—your team will see right through you if you are not authentic (missing your own "ring of truth"), and their lack of trust will continue. Be trustworthy and own up to your own foibles, history, and mistakes. Share all information with the team; when you can't, tell them why. You have to show you trust your team—first.

Give up command-and-control leadership, and stop micromanagement. Telling people to trust one another will not work. Telling people what to do—and, even more importantly, how to do it—also shows a lack of trust. If you trust people, you know they will do what they say they will do and you recognize they know best how to do it. Micromanagement sends a message that you do not trust the people you are managing.

Your leadership will be tested by your team. Team members will come back several times to see if you will rescue them, fix it for them, and tell them what to do and how to do it; if you will really accept mistakes; and whether you genuinely trust them to deliver. They will watch you carefully and test your trustworthiness. Will you listen? Will you give your team members the information they ask for? Will you admit your mistakes? Will you be honest?

Imagine a team where you feel you can always bring up your ideas, and those ideas are well received, heard, and valued—where you feel comfortable in questioning the ideas and logic from everyone on the team, including the leader. In this team, you feel your ideas, when they contribute to the corporate goals and purpose, are implemented. What are the characteristics of this environment? To assist you in forming this image, imagine the opposite situation—an environment where you don't feel you can express your ideas or get them implemented.

### Remove Debilitating Fear

We called it "the Departure Lounge." Anyone who brought bad news to the manager was moved into that office and in three months was no longer with the company.

I landed in the middle of this project by accident and said "yes" because it was a huge challenge—and I like big challenges! With 120 people (60% consultants) and a $120 million budget, we were to build a Swiss electronic stock exchange, one that would move the Swiss traders off the floor and into the electronic age.

Challenges—this project had them in spades. The project had failed twice before—once with a local team and once with a famous consulting firm—and it was now on its way to failing again. Matters were complicated by the fact that every Swiss bank (approximately 50 in total) had financed the project; all of the banks were the project's customers, and all had different requirements, needs, and desires. An electronic stock exchange hadn't been built in 20 years, and an upgrade to other existing systems was drastically needed. Now this extremely high-profile project was way behind schedule. In the existing culture of fear, there seemed little chance for success. Mistakes would be hidden and remain uncorrected, and the system would most likely fail again.

I needed to solve this problem and remove the fear, at least in the teams. I protected each team's boundaries and built confidence with my team leaders by delivering project status information and all the successes to the project leader on a regular basis. We solved the problems of the system with the teams through collaboration. When bad news needed to be delivered, all of the team leaders delivered it together. After all, they couldn't let all of us go. No one ever moved into the Departure Lounge again.

Without ideas from your team, progress will be slow and perhaps impossible. Debilitating fear is what keeps team members from expressing their questions, solutions, analysis, and investigations. They are afraid of humiliation, ridicule, and loss of respect. Their deepest fear? Loss of their position, pay, and perhaps their job. An environment characterized by pervasive fear results in paralysis and catastrophizing (making things seem worse than they are).

Nevertheless, there are certainly ways to mitigate fear. As a leader, you can acknowledge openly with the team the fear that you feel in the team. Imagine, reframe, and describe the team culture as a trusting team. Remind the team members that they have choices in how they respond to the fear. Ask them to give the team a chance and bring their ideas to team meetings or simply try their ideas out on other team members on a one-on-one basis. Practice the steps to change: Celebrate resistance, figure out what to be (not what not to be), and take small steps.

In rapidly changing environments, Warren Bennis notes, people fear losing their identity, losing recognition of their intellectual mastery, and losing their individualism [1]. To reduce this fear, provide positive feedback that is as specific as possible, based on actual results. Positive feedback reduces fear when it is specific, authentic, and based on actual results. There is no such thing as "constructive criticism"—it is a dichotomy. How often when someone says, "I'd like to give you some constructive criticism," do you think the message will be good news? Criticism is not constructive and often instills fear in the person being criticized. Avoid negative feedback and "constructive criticism." Give people continuous feedback that honors the relationship.

Remember, fearless people take on seemingly impossible objectives. They love a challenge and want to make a run at possibilities where they just might succeed.

### *Transparency*

I am puzzled why some leaders continue to think they should be the arbiters of the information each person in the company needs to perform his or her work. When I begin a complex task, I am not sure I have all the information I need. In the U.S. space program, leaders were tasked with putting a man on the moon in 10 years, knowing full well the technology they needed had not been invented yet! Given the complexities of the mind and its network of processing, who knows what small bit of information could trigger a significant innovation, find an error, or discover a solution?

In his book *The Seven-Day Weekend* [5], Ricardo Semler, CEO of Brazilian-based Semco SA, writes that all information should be shared with everyone in the company. He feels that if you don't trust the people in your company to know which information should be kept within the company, why are those people working there? The people in Semler's company decide on their own salary based on three pieces of information: (1) the balance sheet from the business unit where the person works, (2) the salaries everyone in the entire company makes, and (3) a national comparison of their jobs with others within the same industry. In other words, Semco practices full transparency. When important information is withheld from people, the message is that they are not trustworthy or that they aren't intelligent enough to work with all the information. But if they don't have the complete picture, how can they solve problems and maximize opportunities?

Who knows which piece of information could trigger a significant innovation, uncover an expensive error, or discover a breakthrough solution to a chronic problem? If you believe knowledge is power, increase the power of each member of your team—and the team's collective ability to do its best work—by supporting the knowledge base of your organization. Allow the power of information to grow exponentially through transparency.

### *"Communicate? I Already Know That!"*

Communication is perhaps the biggest problem in organizations today. Yes, we have been inundated with the message to communicate and we understand the value of communication as a leader. The message has not escaped any of us—and you don't need to hear more of it from us.

Nevertheless, there is a specific area of communication that has struck a chord in collaborative environments—which may be a different focus. When information is withheld in any communication, that sequestering can be perceived, felt, or interpreted as mistrust. In other words, people feel you are keeping information from them because you don't trust them. Even worse, people can become fearful and begin to imagine team changes, pay cuts, demotions, and layoffs, all because it seemed to the listener that information was left out of the communication. ("Perception is reality.")

We had finally found a good candidate for senior project leader of a high-profile project. The last step was for the candidate to interview with the other three VPs with whom she would be working. The candidate gave us some dates and times, and we agreed to a time. The evening before the meeting I got an email from our candidate: "Something has come up and I need to reschedule." That was all the information I got. I immediately became angry and thought she had a better offer for lunch and was blowing us off. It was not easy to get a time with the other VPs.

This perception led to my thinking that I had picked the wrong person, that she didn't understand the seriousness of the position and our own urgency. I was afraid I had made a mistake and would lose the respect of the other VPs. The next morning, as soon as the day began, our candidate called: "I am so sorry. One of my team leaders is out sick and her release is today. I need to be there to help if I can. I will work around any schedule if that works for you. I can come in at 7 in the morning; I can come after work, or anytime tomorrow. Please let me know what will work for you." I now had *all* the information. My fears and anger disappeared. She was the right candidate.

Err on the side of giving more information than required. Explain why, whenever possible, or at least why you cannot share more information than you have given or was asked for. This may seem like a repeat of the transparency message, but it is a lesson sometimes lacking in our consciousness.

Too often we hear the statement about our colleagues, "They just don't know how to communicate!" You didn't necessarily hire your technical staff for their communication skills (but we hope you did for your marketing and sales staff); you hired them to be good engineers and programmers. Your job as a leader is to learn how to hear them and to communicate so they can hear you.

### Autonomy

Let each person hold himself or herself and that person's team responsible for what he or she controls: effort, performance, honesty, suggestions, and improvements.

People do what they are measured by. Reward innovation, creativity, and imagination (more on this topic in the section on the collaboration process).

## Step 2: Assemble the Right Team of People

"That's not what I wanted!" "I can't sell that!" Marketing folks take one look at the finished product and roll their eyes. Customers can't find the value in the latest upgrade. Users inside your company stumble when using the new systems because they do not fit seamlessly with their workflow. Avoid these missteps by bringing the right people together: marketing, finance, architects, senior developers, and customers. And keep them together, especially when making decisions. Having customers and marketing people collaborate directly with engineers can shorten the decision time and enable you to rapidly incorporate changes that customers and marketing teams feel are needed. Of course, this kind of meeting of the minds should not be attempted without discipline and thought. Decisions must be made based on value, collaboratively, using the decision tools described in Chapter 5.

One of the most well-documented stories of early collaborations was the building of the Boeing 777 [7]. Because they were determined to become a competitive leader in the aeronautical industry, Boeing's teams agreed collaboration would lead to success. The effort ultimately took 5 years and involved 10,000 people. In the course of this venture, one event stands out. As part of the collaboration, Boeing had involved everyone, at some point or another, who would touch the aircraft after it was built. During the design stage, team members talked to a group of runway support teams. One person who drove the airplane refueling truck blurted out, "We can't get the gas up there." The gas cap was in the wrong place. Because it was caught in the design phase, this problem was easy to fix.

Had it not been caught until after the aircraft was built, the issue would have been much harder to solve.

## Step 3: Stimulate the Flow of Ideas Using a Collaborative Process

It is important to think about collaboration in three ways: pushing decisions to the edge of your organization, involving people in decision making, and determining how and where you can use collaboration.

### *Push Decisions to the Edge of Your Organization*

Ralph Stayer, the CEO of Johnsonville Foods, worried whether the people in his company truly cared about the company they worked for. The employees were bored; they came to work halfheartedly and made thoughtless and costly mistakes. They were not taking responsibility for their work. Stayer began to realize that he "couldn't give responsibility; people had to expect it, want it, even demand it" [6]. To address this issue, the line workers were asked to do their own quality control, tasting the foods they made. They also began to answer the customer letters. Performance improved as teams took ownership of their work, began collecting data, and monitoring performance and profits. Even so, a few lackluster performers remained. The line workers looked to senior leadership to "fix it." Instead, the leaders asked themselves who was in the best position to deal with this problem. Their conclusion? The people on the shop floor knew best. The teams took it upon themselves to address performance issues and, in some cases, fired nonperformers. Those closest to the issue made the decisions.

Your employees know which processes are working in your organization and which ones are not. Those personnel working directly with your market will know when changes occur that need attention. You have the best talent; when they solve the problems or find a new direction in which to take your organization, listen to them. Then let them implement the ideas many agree would benefit the company.

After getting the right people to solve a problem or create a new product together, use the following collaboration process to stimulate ideas and capture creative thinking:

- Agree to the goals and objectives.
- Brainstorm all tasks to reach the agreed-upon goals and objectives.
- Group like items together, in silence.

- Prioritize based on value.
- Let people, in a team setting, decide what the team needs to do to reach the goal, and what they, as individuals, want to do and how they want to do it.
- Have the team define success and how it will be measured.

### The Collaboration Process at Work

Suppose productivity in the organization is at a standstill. For example, at the company described at the beginning of this chapter, the organization had reached capacity and could not hire more help. They needed to increase the throughput of projects. How could you find out how your company might increase productivity?

Ask your teams. Bring them together and, armed with a raft of sticky notes and pens, ask the following question: What's not working? Ask each person to write one thing that is not working on one sticky note—as many nonworking items or processes as they can think of, using as many sticky notes as possible. Invite each person, one at a time, to read his or her notes aloud and put the notes on the wall. Then comes the hard part: Every person is to come up to the wall and, *in silence,* group the sticky notes. (It is interesting to see who breaks the rule first and to see how long it takes for the group to begin to nonverbally collaborate.) After they have grouped all of the notes, work together to name each group of notes and put the title on another sticky note near the group.

Next, prioritize. People do what they are passionate about. Think about your own to-do list. Are you passionate about completing the items that keep falling to the bottom of your list? Likewise, to collaborate successfully, we need to find out what the team is passionate about. Add up the number of groups, divide by 3, and round up the answer. The result is the number of votes each person has. For example, if there are 16 groups, each person would have 6 votes. Individuals can cast all their votes for one group if they like—a weighted voting system.

Ask each person to vote for things that are "not working" the most. If you worry about your influence over this process, step outside the room while they vote. The final step is to form small teams, with each team selecting a different topic in the most voted-for categories. Teams should then develop strategies and actions to "fix," correct, or improve what is not working. After each team has presented its "how to" solutions to the entire group, a discussion should be held to unearth any other ideas. Then, ask for volunteers to lead the effort to correct the nonworking items—and have them commit to a date by which they will have the task done. Be clear that they do not have to work alone, but that they will be responsible for leading the effort to completion.

Talented people don't like to be given orders. Instead, they prefer to make a commitment and keep it. They enjoy making meaningful contributions not just related to what you already know they know, but also in terms of new ideas.

### Using the Collaboration Process

There are many ways to use this process:

- Gather leaders together and identify your purpose, differentiation factors, and decision filters; determine what goes on your billboard; and answer the Five Questions to check your strategy (see Chapter 2).
- Determine the complexity and uncertainty factors that you want to manage (see Chapter 4).
- Find the consideration and benefits you need to build your decision model (see Chapter 5).
- Determine the projects you need to reach your purpose and goals.
- Identify the value of ideas you may want to implement.

Use this process for answering any questions that need more minds than one for their solution (when is this *not* true?), for bringing together disgruntled people who don't understand why one idea is better than another, for revisiting processes that persist only because "that's how we have always done it," and for deciding where the company should go next and how to get there.

The collaboration process is an excellent means of discovering issues and areas that need addressing in your organization and in your marketplace. Solving these problems can be accomplished in many ways; this process is only one approach.

## Step 4: Stand Back and Let People Work

This topic is a tool for both collaborating and leading collaboration efforts. You will find the tools for standing back in the next section. Read on!

# Leading Collaboration

People need leaders, especially in collaboration. Unfortunately, leaders all too often "step" on the progress of the team in their own collaboration. Leading collaboration is a four-step process:

1. Get the right people.
2. Trust first!
3. Let people collaborate to determine the direction of your organization, including how to get there and how success is defined.
4. Stand back and let people work.

## Step 1: Get the Right People

Getting the right people involves putting a great team together by assessing the values, abilites, and interests of potential team members.

### Put a Great Team Together

"What do you do, Pollyanna?" I was at an intake interview to volunteer for a nonprofit organization; I was the volunteer.

"I'm a leader of large-scale projects."

"What do you like about what you do?"

"I love to make sure the team members have a clear idea of what they want to achieve, and I want to make sure they have everything they need to succeed. I like to work with teams—to lead teams."

I was a bit tenuous in my response. The last time I volunteered, things didn't go so well. I sat in a park and collected signatures from people. It was a worthwhile effort, but we did not have the supplies we needed, signs arrived too late, and the relief team did not show up. Overall, the experience was disappointing and felt like a waste of time.

"We need a volunteer's policy and procedure manual. We have several people who want to help, but we need a team leader. What about helping with that?"

I jumped at the opportunity. It was a great experience: The team was good fun and worked hard. We delivered a 40-page document covering all the needed policies and procedures for the volunteers in the organization. Other nonprofits have since asked for copies and put the manual to use with minor changes. Along the way, I learned that people do what they are passionate about, especially volunteers. Also, people want to do something they are good at, to contribute their expertise and knowledge. They want to do work that makes a difference, work that matters. This is true in all organizations, whether for profit or not for profit.

What makes for a great team? When all members have their own passions about their work, know what they do best, and understand how they contribute to the company's goals and objectives. When team members operate where these three areas intersect (see Figure 3.1), you have the best team. Similar to Jim Collins's model [3] for company goals, I model my own experiences for individuals, providing a tool for determining what each person wants to do.

You also need to be operating in this intersection, at all times. This requirement operates as a filter for the activities you take on. It provides a basis for determining how you can best contribute to an organization and how interested you might be.

I use this idea as a filter for all the opportunities that come my way. As a guest lecturer at a university in its leadership classes for the executive master's programs, I was once asked by the administration to teach an

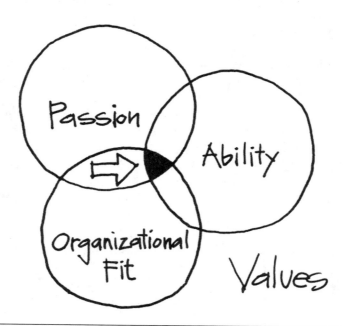

**FIGURE 3.1** Personal filters

algebra class. Yes, I do have a degree in math and I like to teach. But I am no longer passionate about the subject of mathematics. My passion is now focused on leadership—so I turned down the offer (no intersection with passion).

I also would not need a doctor on an architecture project, unless I was building a hospital or medical clinic (no organizational fit). I am passionate about art, but I am terrible at it. So I leave the artistic work to the artists, and I enjoy their work whenever I can (no ability).

### Look at a Person's Values First

A stack of résumés sits in front of you. You've read them and sorted them. You think you've found candidates who would likely fit into your company, but you want the best people in your company. So how do you decide among these applicants? How do you find the "right" people? What do you look for in your new hires? Who will help you gain the innovative edge?

The process unfolds like this: Leaders must trust people so they can stand back and let them innovate. You need to have people in your organization you can trust. As Dee Hock, former CEO of Visa International, suggests:

> Hire and promote first on the basis of integrity; second, motivation; third, capacity; fourth, understanding; fifth, knowledge; and last and least, experience. Without integrity, motivation is dangerous; without motivation, capacity is impotent; without capacity, understanding is limited; without understanding, knowledge is meaningless; without knowledge, experience is blind. Experience is easy to provide and quickly put to good use by people with the other qualities [8].

Most people approach this task in the opposite order, putting experience first. Conventional interviews target knowledge and experience, but these facets alone won't deliver the caliber of employees or staffing we want for creative projects and innovative organizations. They are the easiest characteristics to ask about (and for the interviewee to discuss), yet they are the last two qualities on Hock's list. Managers fall back on them because they don't know how to interview for characteristics that are more difficult to document on a résumé.

In addition to the qualities on Hock's list, look for attitude, talent, intelligence, and authenticity when hiring team members. In a collaborative environment, people need to be able to handle nondirective leadership and not expect leaders to have all the answers. Hire people who can champion their ideas, take ownership, and live with change and uncertainty. Seek a level of maturity and/or willingness to learn that doesn't necessarily correspond to the number of years in a job role. All of these qualities fuel creativity and innovation.

Why is integrity so important? Have you ever worked with someone who is lying to you or to others in your company? Here, we don't mean grandiosity or exaggeration; we mean not telling the truth. How motivated were you to work for that person? And didn't you question his or her motivation? Did you think the individual was putting the purpose of your organization above his or her personal agenda? Was there a nagging doubt in the back of your mind about everything that person suggested or did?

## Step 2: Trust First!

Leaders must trust the people they work with. In addition, they must earn the trust of their peers and team members. From the moment individuals become members of your team, trust them and demonstrate your trust. Set the example of trustworthiness by admitting mistakes, apologizing when needed, and operating with integrity. Remember what Ricardo Semler says: "If you cannot trust the employees in your organization to know what information they can share outside your company and what they cannot, why are they in your company?" [5]. Hire the very best people and then trust them.

Remember, "suspicion is a permanent condition" [2]. How would someone prove to you that he or she is trustworthy? What would it take?

I had gone to Switzerland as a database consultant to build control systems for electrical power plants. When I came on board, the company was building systems with fixed-price contracts that should take one year to deliver but the jobs were taking four years! This business model was very broken. It was quite a situation. Within four months, I was running the team. However, I had no power to hire and fire anyone, I could give no one a raise, I was a consultant, I was a foreigner, and I was a woman in a country that gave women the vote in '73—and that's not 1873, but rather 1973! I got the teams together, asked the members what needed to be done to deliver, and let them decide what to do and how to do it.

"How do you want me to build this?" Jan, one of the team members, was at my desk the day after the meeting to decide who did what by when.

"How do *you* want to build it?" I replied.

The next morning, Jan was at my desk. "How should I design this?" he asked.

"What do you think is the best design?" I answered.

The next morning, again, he was at my desk! "So, how would you like me to build this?"

"Jan, we hired you for your expertise. Give it your best shot. I'm here if you need anything." And off he went. I saw Jan working in the teams, collaborating. But he never asked for help, and I had to keep stepping back. If I asked if he needed anything, I was fearful my questioning would suggest that I did not trust him. The "drumbeat" said he was doing fine. Each time the system was integrated, his portion had the smallest number of errors.

By letting people choose what they wanted to do and how to do it, in the two years I was there, we managed to deliver eight systems.

Choice is not only a positive motivator; it gives people ownership. They want to deliver to on their own commitments. And it also provides accountability—specifically, self-accountability.

As an executive, I was asked to lead a project that the company president had mentioned four times in the annual report as representing the future of the organization. The sales people were out selling it, but development had not begun. On my first day I found four team leaders waiting for directions.

"What do we need to build? Where is the feature list?" I was met with blank stares. Not a good start.

"We don't have one."

"Okay, who would like to put one together?"

"I will," John spoke up.

"How long will it take you?"

"Six weeks." We would modify 20 systems. This seemed about right to me.

"Great!" The weeks progressed. John reported steady progress in every standup meeting. I offered my help and always got an "I'm okay" answer. On the due date I got a half-page of features! The book the sales people were using to sell the system was 3 inches thick! I turned on my heels, went down to personnel, and had John taken off the team. This was not a mistake; this was not delivering. John had decided what and when to deliver but did not deliver. As Jim Collins would say, he was off the bus [3]. Had John volunteered that things were not going well, the team could have pitched in and helped. The real issue was, could he be trusted again?

## Step 3: Let the Team Decide the Direction of the Company

What should the company take on? Which strategy will work best? Use collaboration to discover, from the teams and divisions closest to your marketplace, where the organization should focus next. Today, no one person can possibly know enough to make these decisions alone.

Through collaboration, you can involve all the thinkers and take advantage of all the experience in your organization. Build business value models together, balance your portfolios as a team, develop options for maximizing value, and avoid the cost of delay. Build strategies throughout the entire organization in collaboration.

## Step 4: Stand Back and Let People Work

From my first day as a developer, leaders continually asked me to do things that I knew were a waste of time, keeping me from getting the "real" work done. When I became a project manager, those leaders continued wasting my time with endless questions: "Where are we? When will we finish? How many errors are there? What are you going to deliver? How much will it cost? Why are you doing it that way?" "Endless" is the right term here—their questions seemed to stretch to infinity. But when I became the "dreaded" leader, their motives became crystal clear. There are things leaders need to know when developing products that meet customer needs in the optimal market window so the company can continue to exist and, ideally, prosper.

Leaders can stifle progress when they interfere with team processes. At the same time, as a leader, you don't want an on-track project to go over the cliff and deliver the wrong results. There are times when leaders should stand back and let the team work, and times when they should step up and lead. The result: the leadership "two step" (see Figure 3.2). But how do we decide which time is which?

Let's start with standing back. You have great talent in your organization. You hired your staff for their ability to address issues, solve problems, and create innovative and competitive products to make your company successful. Put them to work improving operations, increasing workflow, and removing bottlenecks. Your employees operate closest to the problems and have the best chance of finding workable solutions. You hired these people to deliver new, exciting, and competitive products to the marketplace before your competition could. You need their creativity, their thinking, and their ability to innovate if your company is to thrive.

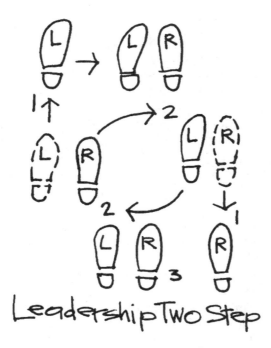

**FIGURE 3.2**   Leadership "two step"

As their leader, you must unleash this talent and allow your people to succeed. Create an environment based on trust; bring together people who have the right knowledge; ensure they understand the objectives, purpose, and constraints (e.g., budget, market windows) of the project; and then stand back.

As contributing team members, we want to take pride in our work; we want to use our knowledge and experience to develop and deliver our assigned part of the product. We want to own our part and we want to create the best and most efficient solution. And we want to collaborate with our team to make sure we all deliver our parts by assisting one another when we need it. We are not happy when someone begins to tell us how we should do our job or when we don't get the opportunity to find and correct our own mistakes. After all, that's how we learn and gain more experience and knowledge. Clearly, we need leaders to stand back and let us get the work done.

What about accountability? We want to be held accountable by the people who understand what we are doing, who understand how we think, and who share in the challenges of the team. In other words, we want our teammates to hold us accountable—and they do.

But there are times when leaders need to step up and lead. Leaders must make sure their projects and teams do not go off the cliff. As leaders, we want effective projects to deliver results. But we do not want just any result; we want the *right* results—results that are in line with the corporate strategy. You could just lecture your teams on this topic and hope they get it. More effective than lecturing, however, is asking questions to help them discover the answers for themselves: "How does this feature/objective fit with our company strategy? If it does not, do we need to modify our strategy? Does our prioritization scheme match our business priorities? Can we reach our market window?" Project leaders, product leaders, and corporate leaders should be asking such questions continuously.

Allow your teams to manage their workload, find solutions, and deliver them. Make sure that all team members understand that their solutions, objectives, and goals must be in line with the company strategy. Help your teams find their own solutions, but only after they have made valiant attempts on their own. Don't give them solutions, but rather ask questions without giving answers. Your questions will help them discover their solutions. Use your questions to unleash the talent and creativity in your organization, and then stand back, get out of the way, and let them get the "real" work done.

## Tools for Stepping Up

Now, let's take a look at when leaders should lead and how they do so without crushing collaboration, adding fear, or demotivating the team:

- Keep the team focused (or refocused).
- Expect success—but allow mistakes.
- Base measurements on team results.
- Take the "fun" out of being dysfunctional.

### Keep the Focus

Set the goal clearly. On Apollo 13, mission leader Gene Kranz made the call to shut down the command module, which ruled out landing on the moon. "Forget the flight plan," ordered Kranz. "From this moment on, we are improvising a new mission. How do we get our men home?"

Teams don't get to do whatever they want, whenever they want. But they do need time for exploration of their ideas and possible solutions.

When chaos has gone on too long, step in and ask questions to help the team get back on track. Ask—don't tell. The team does not need to be told in which direction to go; they need assistance in discovering their own direction as it relates to their current project.

Remember the purpose, benefits, and constraints discussed in building your decision model (see Chapter 5). Ask questions about the teams' activities, what considerations they took into account, and how their activities meet the purpose defined in that model.

### Expect Success—But Allow Mistakes

We were two weeks away from the week-long site acceptance test for the first major upgrade of an electrical control system. I walked into the test lab, looked around at the chaos, and panicked. I knew exactly what the team of 40 people needed to do to create a successful test, and I opened my mouth to speak. Fortunately, I stopped in time. I realized that I might possibly "save" the team from failure—but in doing so, I would also take away their chance to succeed on their own. I turned on my heels, left the lab, and never went in there again. Two weeks later, the team finished the test in four days, one day early. The success was theirs, not mine.

When leading collaboration, you need to step aside and let the people in your organization do their work. You do trust them, right?

Stress the motto, "Fail early—fail fast!" People learn from their mistakes. Right now, your team may be worried about taking a risk and failing. To be sure, removing disruptive fear will help. But your most important contribution is to protect both your team members *and* your organization. Create a way for the team to fail safely. What does that mean? First, you don't want them to be embarrassed in front of your customers, in front of organizational leaders, and in front of other teams. Add a step in the processes (or, better still, suggest that the team members evaluate the possibility of adding a step) where they can walk through their results before the results go outside of their team.

### Base Measurements on Team Results

People do what they are measured by. If you ask people to come to work at 8 in the morning and go home at 5, will you get 40 hours of results? Not always—actually, not often. I have seen some companies take this tack and get only 20% productivity (results)!

The largest user challenge for the Swiss electronic stock exchange was moving the traders from the floor to electronic workstations. The learning curve would be steep. Most importantly, the users had to have what they needed on day one.

The workstation development team formed a focus group of floor traders and built four prototypes. After each effort, the team leader would say, "Don't worry, Pollyanna—there's code in here we can reuse."

It didn't matter to me. I didn't care if they reused any code. My response was always the same: "I care about only one thing. When the system goes live, I don't want any traders to throw their workstations out the window." The system has been up and running for more than 12 years and not one workstation has gone out a window.

### Take the "Fun" Out of Being Dysfunctional

Ignore unprofessional behavior.

Asked to help staff and board members collaborate on taking their library to the next level, I was not sure what to expect. Would they be strict taskmasters or gentle nurturing participants? (Which kind of librarian do you remember from school?) I presented the tools for collaboration and we had a break. The board president approached me and said, "I am surprised that you don't address diversity in your model." It was a rhetorical question because the model was totally inclusive: Everyone is heard during the brainstorming and voting techniques. I did not move a muscle and did not say one word. I stared at him as if he had not said anything.

The board president tried again at lunch with another question, equally as rhetorical. He was looking for an argument that he felt he could win, and that would be a distraction from the work at hand. Again, I ignored him. After lunch, in the brainstorming session, he refused to participate. I stood behind a bookcase and in a low voice, said, "Be a sport. We need your input." He did not even get recognition from my body language and presence. He stopped his obstructive behavior and made valuable contributions for the rest of the day.

What do you do about those people who are "gaming the system," where team members leverage the leader in an attempt to discredit a team member? This kind of bad behavior does not often arise in a "healthy" team—one whose members work collaboratively, understand and respect one another's contributions, remain focused, and demonstrate ownership. But you don't have that, at least not yet. To get there, take the "fun" out of being dysfunctional. Remove the reward people are getting for nonprofessional behavior within the team. When someone causes distractions, such as asking rhetorical questions with no real purpose—where the person is trying to impress you with the "right answer" or embarrass you if you made a mistake—ignore this behavior. Stand quietly and do not say a word. Alternatively, look to others in the room and change the subject. Remember, negative attention can be a reward.

## What Is Your Leadership "Tipping Point"

Find your leadership "tipping point"—the point where you discover when to lead and when to step back. Ask yourself what contribution you might make or whether the team might discover more without you. What is your agenda to engage with the team? Do you trust the team members to reach their goals without your guidance? We discuss this topic in more detail in Chapter 6.

## Putting These Tools to Work

"How do I get started?"

Take a look at your environment. Is it open? If your team has any of the following characteristics, it is not open:

- Fear: People are afraid to speak up, afraid to fail, afraid of humiliation.
- Secrecy, territoriality, or everyone-out-for-themselves attitude: Members of the team pontificate and spout monologues while keeping valuable information to themselves.
- Lack of engagement: Team members do not support one another, missing out on participation in team discussions and decisions.
- Defensive and negative attitudes: Team members exhibit closed body language, never saying a good word about other team members or the tasks at hand.
- Judgmental and condescending attitudes: Ideas are dismissed without consideration or criticized unfairly.
- Passive-aggressive behavior and lack of integrity: In meetings, people agree to one thing; outside the meetings, they say and do another.

- Lack of patience and tendency toward agitation: There is tension in every working encounter, yet at the same time team members lack initiative.
- Rampant gossip and complaints: Team members talk behind one anothers' backs; they use mean-spirited humor instead of healthy, fun humor.

Do a check just in case. Bring the team together. Use the collaboration process to answer the following question: "Which characteristics make up an open environment?" Make sure the team groups the characteristics in silence. Then, as they vote, you might want to leave the room. Tally the totals. The most important characteristic, as chosen by voters, is usually the one thing the team's current environment is lacking.

Next, break up the group into small teams and develop strategies and action items based on how you will fill the gaps in your environment to make it open. Develop an action plan by letting team members volunteer to implement strategies.

This question may not be concrete enough to start. Maybe you need a "safe" topic first. What about an upcoming project? Relevant questions to pursue might include these options:

- What is the purpose of this project?
- What is the scope?
- What are the required features? Nice-to-have features? The wish list?
- What are the value inputs of making project decisions?
- What are the best methods to use, and who is the best leader?

On the other side, take on the corporate goals and objectives:

- How can we reach the goals we are responsible for?
- What are the value inputs to making decisions?
- Which strategies will work best?
- Which processes need to be fixed, abandoned, or created?
- How can we increase our throughput?

Make sure action item lists include due dates determined by the people who volunteered to own the action item. Also, don't let people volunteer other people to handle action items. Ask questions, and don't give the answers or otherwise rescue the team. The members will find their way and their own answers. Decide, as a team, how members will hold one another accountable and how to measure success.

## Summary

To collaborate:

- Create an open environment that fosters innovation, creativity, and the free flow of ideas.
- Bring the right experience and talent together to address the issue or problem or just to do some thinking.
- Use the collaboration process for the discovery of ideas.
- Stand back and let the team work.

To use the collaboration process:

- Agree to the goals and objectives.
- Brainstorm using sticky notes and pens.
- Group in silence.
- Prioritize using a weighted voting process (number of groups, divide by 3, and round up the answer).
- Find strategies and action items.
- Let people volunteer for the action items and determine their due date.

To lead collaboration:

- Trust first! Trust the people in your company by hiring them based on integrity and passion for the work done in your company.
- Listen to suggestions about the direction in which people feel the company should go.
- Stand aside and support employees' efforts in the pursuit of the ideas to make your company great.

Other tools discussed in this chapter:

- Stand back. Trust first; let people choose what to do, how, and by when; guide through questions (ask, don't tell); and ask the team to hold each other accountable.

- Step up. Keep the team focused (or refocused); expect success, but allow mistakes; base measurements on team results; take the "fun" out of being dysfunctional.
- Find your own leadership "tipping point."

As a leader, keep the following concepts in mind:

- Ensure all members of your organization have everything they need to succeed.
- Create an environment that is so stimulating and rewarding that people would want to work with you, even if they did not have to.
- "People don't resist change; they resist being changed" [4].

If you focus on these concepts and operate with integrity, you cannot fail.

# References

[1] Bennis, Warren. *Beyond Bureaucracy: Essays on the Development and Evolution of Human Organization*. San Francisco: Jossey-Bass, 1993.

[2] Buckingham, Marcus, and Coffman, Curt. *First, Break All the Rules: What the World's Greatest Managers Do Differently*. New York: Simon & Schuster, 1999.

[3] Collins, Jim. *Good to Great: Why Some Companies Make the Leap . . . and Others Don't*. New York: HarperBusiness, 2001.

[4] Scholtes, Peter R., Joiner, Brian L., and Streibel, Barbara J. *The Team Handbook*. Madison, WI: Oriel, 2003.

[5] Semler, Ricardo. *The Seven-Day Weekend: Changing the Way Work Works*. New York: Portfolio, 2004.

[6] Slayer, Ralph. "How I Learned to Let My Workers Lead." *Harvard Business Review*, November–December 1990, pp. 32–41.

[7] Sabbagh, Karl. *21st Century Jet: Building of 777*. 285 min. Skyscraper Productions, 1996.

[8] Waldrop, M. Mitchell. "Dee Hock on Management." *Fast Company*, October 5, 1996.

# CHAPTER 4

# DELIVERY

## The Big Ideas

- By understanding the uncertainty and complexity characteristics of your projects, you can identify better ways to lead those projects.
- High complexity or uncertainty correlates to higher risk. Reduce these factors, and you reduce your level of risk. Project decomposition can reduce complexity, while incremental delivery helps lead a project through uncertainty.
- Some leaders are natural managers of complexity, while others are experts at uncertainty. Match leadership styles to project characteristics, and develop leaders' skills to broaden their capabilities.

## Case Study: The Swiss Stock Exchange

The Swiss stock exchange was preparing to enter electronic trading. There had been two prior attempts to develop the software solutions. The first attempt was an internal development effort, and it failed. In the second attempt, the project was outsourced to a prominent consulting firm; it failed as well. In both of these prior failures, everyone thought that they were doing things by the book using software development best practices.

The third attempt was getting under way and there were real concerns about the prospects for yet another failure. Pollyanna got involved on the team and eventually ended up leading the project. The challenges were significant. The team consisted of more than 120 people, and 60% of those were contractors. There were multiple customers, as every Swiss bank (approximately 50 in total) had financed the project, and each bank had different requirements and desires. The existing systems were 20 years old and upgrades were drastically needed. Clearly, this was a very high-profile project with a lot of money at stake.

On the positive side, the project attracted the best talent and was able to specify its delivery date within a reasonable time frame. The 2-second throughput requirement, total software and hardware redundancy, and "lights out" maintenance model all seemed doable. A retired trader was heading up the functional specification team—a sort of on-site "customer." Things looked better than before.

But there were other ominous signs that history would repeat itself. The team in charge of building one of the key server-side components had developed a two-year plan detailing tasks down to the level of every 15 minutes. What were they thinking? Creation of such a schedule is over-planning even for a project with almost no uncertainty. The team leaders had fallen into the trap of the illusion of control—even though they actually had almost *no* control. Instead, they spent an inordinate amount of time updating the detailed plan and trying to justify how they would get back on schedule.

Pollyanna had the team members move to a system that would allow them to update and reprioritize the features and the work tasks on a weekly basis. The team leaders reviewed progress at the end of each week and then, based on this information, reprioritized the next week's work. Every six weeks, the teams re-estimated and re-planned tasks for the next three-month iterative release. Change was inevitable and was managed through the reprioritization process. All team leaders made the decisions together.

Next, Pollyanna worked with the trading system team to build the workstation where the traders would make their trades and gather information. The trading system was associated with a lot more uncertainty because it was brand new and would be more intimately connected to the end users. To get it right, the developers formed a user group of traders and built prototypes to obtain useful feedback. It took four prototypes to get a system that the users liked—but what really mattered is that the users were happy with the final delivery.

Together, this team of teams successfully delivered the first fully computerized stock exchange system integrating trading, clearing, settlement, and member back-offices.

## All Projects Are Not Created Equal

Leaders are constantly hoping to find the magic project management approach that will guarantee successful delivery of their projects. But what any experienced project manager knows is that all projects are not created equal; as a consequence, no single approach can possibly be appropriate for all projects. Certainly, many good techniques and practices are applicable to a large collection of projects, but the idea of running projects "by the book" is a mirage. While all projects are different, certain patterns can be discerned among projects with similar characteristics. For those projects with similar characteristics, certain approaches to leadership and governance work especially well.

The two primary characteristics that influence and drive project management characteristics are complexity and uncertainty. *Complexity* is a measure of the size of the project, the dependencies of the project, and the nature of the project team. *Uncertainty* is an indicator of what is known and what is not known about the project; it can include shifts in either the customer needs or the technological implementation. Relatively simple projects with low uncertainty are quite different from highly complex projects with high uncertainty and should be led and managed accordingly.

The 2 × 2 matrix in Figure 4.1 shows the Context Leadership Model for using project complexity and uncertainty to help project leaders guide and govern their projects. Each quadrant is explained in more detail in the sections that follow.

**FIGURE 4.1**  Context Leadership Model

## Sheepdogs: Simple Projects with Low Uncertainty

The easiest and most controllable projects are the simple projects being developed by small teams. All projects have some degree of complexity and uncertainty, but projects categorized in the sheepdog quadrant have the lowest degree of complexity and uncertainty. The idea of the sheepdog is meant to be seen in a positive light: With care and feeding, the sheepdog is very productive. With these types of projects, the best thing to do is to make sure the team knows what is needed and to then stand back and let the team members do their jobs to ship the result. For those projects that have some uncertainty, it is good practice to keep their duration short or to deliver the results in incremental iterations to limit the uncertainty's impact. Prototype or skunkworks projects can also fit in this category. For projects in this quadrant, additional process ceremony and documentation are unnecessary and inefficient, so run them using only the minimal core set of practices used for all projects in all quadrants.

## Colts: Simple Projects with High Uncertainty

New products and initiatives will often have both market and technical uncertainty. If you keep the team small and its members close together, they can react quickly to adapt to those uncertainties. The metaphor of the young colt aptly describes these projects. Colt projects are just getting started and have a lot of energy and freedom. Software projects in these categories are excellent candidates for applying prototyping and light-weight agile development techniques such as Scrum, Extreme Programming, or Crystal. We do not imply that agile practices are applicable only to colts, but rather suggest that colts are particularly well suited to agile approaches.

Because these projects have little complexity, process ceremony and documentation should be kept to the minimal set needed by the team to be effective. The real focus of the team and its leadership needs to be on navigating and managing the uncertainties, with continual and rapid feedback being a key to project success. This type of effort usually requires a leader who has a strong connection to the source of the uncertainty. If the source of the uncertainty lies in the market or the business, then the leader will need to have the appropriate skills and background to deal with those uncertainties. If the uncertainty is primarily technical in nature, then it is a good idea to have a technical leader for the project. In many cases, both technical and market sophistication are needed; if these capabilities are not available in a single leader, the team might need two leaders who will collaborate closely.

## Cows: Complex Projects with Low Uncertainty

The mature systems and product suites that are important to the business will continue to warrant the services of large project teams and are usually the organization's cash cows. In addition to the obvious connection, the cow is a good metaphor for these projects because cows are quite large but don't move particularly fast. Cow projects have less need for agile steering; in fact, they might need disciplined change control on more rigorous requirements or specifications to reduce their impact when many projects or customers depend on them. Projects in this quadrant might aim to be agile enough to respond to some uncertainties, but they need defined and published interfaces to the projects that depend on them.

Cow projects also require more direct project and program management, including looking at issues such as cross-team communication and critical paths. It is common practice for a cow to be an integration project involving a number of smaller projects (typically sheepdogs). Successful leadership of cow projects requires strong skills in working with people and teams and the ability to coordinate the activities of those people and teams.

## Bulls: Complex Projects with High Uncertainty

Projects that are highly complex and have high uncertainty are particularly challenging. Because of the high level of uncertainty, they need to embrace change through iterative feedback to be agile enough to navigate the uncertainty. To run successfully, they require much of the agile steering required for colts, yet also require much of the same process ceremony we use with cows. Communication channels for these projects must be very efficient.

The bull metaphor is quite appropriate for such projects. Bull projects are large and can get out of control quickly if the team isn't careful. They have high visibility throughout the organization, because they often deal with emerging products or initiatives that require significant investment. Often they are next-generation products or solutions that have great hopes to supplant existing cash cows. Expectations are high, yet uncertainty and complexity are equally high.

Leading a bull project is neither easy nor a task for the faint of heart. It is critical that bull projects have the best and most seasoned leaders who understand how to work with agility while cutting through complexity, balancing the dichotomy. These leaders need to have the ability to understand the business and the technology so as to manage the uncertainty, while at the same time being experts at project mechanics and at dealing with the complexities of coordinating people, teams, and across-team activities.

Most organizations have only a few leaders with the requisite capacity to lead such projects. It's unwise for an organization to have more bull projects than project managers who are capable of running bull projects.

# Assessing Project Uncertainty and Complexity

We have introduced this model into a number of organizations. In each case, the organization has ultimately tailored the model to better meet its needs. Some organizations have taken the base model and tweaked it just a bit to fit their needs. Others have bypassed any scoring for the assessment and gotten value out of the model simply by assessing complexity and uncertainty through intuition. At the other extreme, organizations that have a history of detailed process have taken the overall concept and created what we would consider to be a rather complicated scoring model to assess complexity and uncertainty (20–30 attributes for each).

Use whatever scheme works for you. In the base scoring model, we suggest using 1 for low complexity/uncertainty, 3 for medium complexity/uncertainty, and 9 for high complexity/uncertainty. We then suggest using a simple arithmetic average or, if you are feeling more ambitious, a weighted average. Projects scoring greater than about 4 are considered "high complexity/uncertainty."

## Complexity Drivers

The project's structure determines its complexity, which affects the ease or difficulty the team has navigating through the project. Higher complexity implies the need for more structured communication and documentation. In contrast, lower-complexity projects can often thrive on informal communication channels. The parameters and scoring model for the base model are summarized in Table 4.1 and explained in more detail in the sections that follow.

### Team Size

A large team generally implies a complex project. Although situations do arise in which portions of the work are decoupled, with many projects the need for cross-project communication is critical. The number of potential communications interactions goes up exponentially as more members are added to a

**Table 4.1**  Complexity Attributes

| Attribute | Low Complexity (1) | Medium Complexity (3) | High Complexity (9) |
|---|---|---|---|
| Team size | 2 | 15 | 100 |
| Mission critical | Speculative | Established market | Safety critical or significant monetary exposure |
| Team location | Same room | Within same building | Multisite, worldwide |
| Team maturity | Established team of experts | Mixed team of experts and novices | New team of mostly novices |
| Domain knowledge gaps | Developers know the domain as well as expert users | Developers require some domain assistance | Developers have no idea about the domain |
| Dependencies | No dependencies | Some dependencies | Tight integration with several projects |

team. If a team must be large, it is wise to consider subdividing the team at loosely coupled interfaces to allow the subteams to act efficiently.

### Mission and Safety Criticality

If the project puts lives or business-critical functions at risk, we must treat it differently than if the only cost of failure is the project investment. A project with a higher element of criticality will mean greater visibility or exposure for the organization. As such, it requires a more well-defined process for tracking and managing the project and the risks, which ultimately adds to the complexity of the project.

### Team Location

Having everyone in the same room enables high-bandwidth communication among the project team members. A widely distributed team, or one in which a significant portion of the team is located several time zones apart, can significantly increase project complexity. Team location can be a difficult attribute to assess, because use of a team that has one or a few dispersed members may or may not drastically increase the complexity of the project. We've advised teams to use their judgment on this assessment.

### Team Maturity

An established team of experts who have been working together for years on product-line enhancements can almost anticipate what team members are likely to need and do. This kind of "mind reading" contrasts with the situation faced by a brand-new team of relative novices. The latter team requires far more hand holding and guidance, usually in the form of more formalized documentation of requirements and specifications.

### Domain Knowledge Gaps

Many development projects have complex business processes that must be understood at a certain level by everyone on the team. At a minimum, it is critical that the product team have full-time access to the domain specialists to resolve ambiguities and produce the desired product. We've found that this process is greatly simplified when the developers are domain specialists themselves but becomes much more complex when access to domain knowledge is limited.

### Dependencies

In general, the more dependencies that a project has on other projects or third parties, the more complex the project will be. It is critical to manage those dependencies and to track the activities of others so as to create alignment. Sometimes, however, an established third-party dependency does not add greatly to complexity if the team has a consistent track record of working with stable interfaces.

## Uncertainty Drivers

The needs of the customers and the choice of technology are the two major drivers of uncertainty for a project. Higher uncertainty implies the need for a means of absorbing changes and adapting to those changes, with the idea of getting to the ideal solution at the end of the project, though it may not necessarily be the solution that was envisioned at the beginning of the project. The parameters and scoring of the base model are explained in the following sections and summarized in Table 4.2.

**Table 4.2**  Uncertainty Attributes

| Attribute | Low Uncertainty (1) | Medium Uncertainty (3) | High Uncertainty (9) |
|---|---|---|---|
| Market uncertainty | Known deliverable, possibly defined contractual obligation | Initial guess of market target is likely to require steering | New market that is unknown and untested |
| Technical uncertainty | Enhancements to existing architecture | We're not quite sure if we know how to build it | New technology, new architecture; some research may be required |
| Number of customers | Internal customer or one well-defined customer | Multiple internal or small number of defined customers | Shrink-wrapped software |
| Project duration | 0–3 months | 3–12 months | >12 months |
| Approach to change | Significant control over change | Moderate control over change | Embrace or create change |

### Market Uncertainty

If the market or customer needs are well known, the project probably won't need much steering. Conversely, if the customer needs aren't well understood and can be discovered only during the development of the solution, the ability to steer the project to the discovered goal—rather than to the initially stated objective—will be critical.

### Technical Uncertainty

Mature products using proven technology don't involve much technical uncertainty. Sometimes, however, a project may experience uncertainty while rolling out proven technologies that are new to the organization or to the team. By comparison, project teams building new products often want to use the latest technology, so these projects will have a high degree of technical uncertainty.

### Number of Customers

One primary amplifier of market uncertainty relates to the number of customers. A project in which there is one customer who is internal to the organization is quite different from a project in which there are multiple customers with multiple voices. Two issues arise with this attribute. First is the addition of multiple voices, which creates the potential for conflicting needs and gives rise to one form of uncertainty. Second is the inevitable difference between an internal customer and an external customer, particularly if the external customer is a market and not an explicitly identifiable customer. Many markets are fickle and fraught with uncertainty.

### Project Duration

Niels Bohr and Yogi Berra are both quoted as saying, "It is hard to make predictions, especially about the future." The further out the future is, the greater the chance for technical or market uncertainty to affect it. Iterative and incremental deliveries can play a big role in minimizing the risk of uncertainty in projects with a long duration.

### Approach to Change

The approach that the team takes toward managing change indicates how much flexibility the members have in managing uncertainty. For example, some components may be used by a number of other projects. This level of dependency can limit the amount of steering that the other projects can tolerate. While there may be market or technical uncertainty that would suggest a need to absorb change, continually modifying interfaces may not be acceptable when those changes affect other projects.

## Case Study: Integrating Software by Integrating People

By 1996, Landmark Graphics was already a leading provider of software applications in oil and gas exploration. It had grown to this enviable position from a start-up just 15 years earlier. During this time Landmark had expanded its operations via acquisition, resulting in a collection of corporate cultures separated by prior organization, geography, product line, and business domain. At the time, the company had primary development centers in Houston, Austin, Denver, Tulsa, Calgary, and Aberdeen.

In most cases, the software acquired via acquisition was already the market leader. While providing strong technical applications was seen as valuable, the real value proposition to Landmark's customers would come from providing integrated solutions that would substantially improve customer workflows. The company's means of differentiation and purpose were clear. However, each product group had been operating largely independently. There had been some integration activity in the past, but a comprehensive effort would be required to really make integration work.

The overall integration project's complexity attributes are listed in Table 4.3 and the uncertainty attributes in Table 4.4. This effort was clearly a bull program, as it had both high complexity and high uncertainty.

**Table 4.3**   Complexity Attributes

| Attribute | Comments | Score | Graph |
|---|---|---|---|
| Team size | More than 200 | 9 | ■■■■■■■■■ |
| Mission critical | Bet the company | 9 | ■■■■■■■■■ |
| Team location | Distributed worldwide | 9 | ■■■■■■■■■ |
| Team maturity | Established team of experts within their own products | 3 | ■■■ |
| Domain gaps | Some gaps at points of integration | 3 | ■■■ |
| Dependencies | Major dependencies | 9 | ■■■■■■■■■ |

**Table 4.4**   Uncertainty Attributes

| Attribute | Comments | Score | Graph |
|---|---|---|---|
| Market uncertainty | The market was known, but integration at this level had not been done before | 3 | ■■■ |
| Technical uncertainty | The technology was known, but integration at this level had not been done before | 3 | ■■■ |
| Number of customers | Shrink-wrapped software | 9 | ■■■■■■■■■ |

*(continues)*

**Table 4.4**   Uncertainty Attributes *(continued)*

| Attribute | Comments | Score | Graph |
|---|---|---|---|
| Project duration | Approximately 18 months | 9 | ■■■■■■■■■ |
| Change | Integration was the focus; change was inevitable | 3 | ■■■ |

## What the Leaders Did

Several things were done in response to the challenge. First, the CEO of the company and the entire leadership team made it clear that the company's differentiation came from its integrated solutions. They made sure that this mission statement was not just lip service. They made it clear what they wanted and why it was important. Everyone in the company knew what the number one focus was and why it mattered to the company and to its customers. The leadership also reiterated that message on a regular basis. Once the company's focus was clear, a coordinating team was created with the full-time responsibility for bringing the teams together and aligned to the common objective. A senior leader had responsibility for making things happen.

The senior leader recognized that the best way to integrate the software products would be by making sure that the teams and people were better integrated. He took advantage of existing structures of informal communication, such as a weekly all-hands gathering called Friday@4, where people got together for food and drink and checked in on what was happening in the rest of the organization. He also instituted a set of quarterly face-to-face meetings for all the project and product managers and key technical staff. These face-to-face meetings were critical to the success of the integration project. In addition to creating a checkpoint for ensuring that individual projects were on track and providing a venue for sharing learning across the organization, they provided a great forum for getting teams integrated on a social level. These events were always planned to last at least two days and were arranged so that nearly everyone traveled to attend them. As a result, at least one evening was available for the team leaders to socialize on a more informal basis.

The project was an enormous success. Market share grew significantly after the release and solidified Landmark's leadership position as the provider of integrated solutions in oil and gas exploration. In addition, the social bonds continued to flourish and paved the way for further gains in integration in the future.

## Case Study: Time Is on Our Side

In 1998, a software company was facing the Y2K issue. The software that it was producing was mission critical to its customers. The firm needed to protect its customers by ensuring that its software did not have any issues with two-digit years and would not create any work stoppages or incorrect results following the turn of century. Fortunately, the company was able to build on the infrastructure it had put in place to deliver its prior integrated release. However, the new project was a much different program because the focus was on Y2K and Y2K only.

The overall project's complexity attributes are listed in Table 4.5 and the uncertainty attributes in Table 4.6. This overall integration effort was clearly a cow program, with high complexity but low uncertainty.

**Table 4.5**  Complexity Attributes

| Attribute | Comments | Score | Graph |
|-----------|----------|-------|-------|
| Team size | More than 200 | 9 | ■■■■■■■■■ |
| Mission critical | Products are mission critical | 9 | ■■■■■■■■■ |
| Team location | Distributed worldwide | 9 | ■■■■■■■■■ |
| Team maturity | Established team of experts within their own products | 3 | ■■■ |
| Domain gaps | Some gaps at points of integration | 3 | ■■■ |
| Dependencies | Major dependencies | 9 | ■■■■■■■■■ |

**Table 4.6** Uncertainty Attributes

| Attribute | Comments | Score | Graph |
|-----------|----------|-------|-------|
| Market uncertainty | Only Y2K | 1 | ■ |
| Technical uncertainty | Only Y2K | 1 | ■ |
| Number of customers | Many customers, but only one well-defined requirement | 3 | ■■■ |
| Project duration | Approximately 6 months | 3 | ■■■ |
| Change | Eliminate any change other than Y2K issues | 1 | ■ |

## What the Leaders Did

This approach to guiding the program worked very well to accomplish the objective. The approach to change was critical to keeping the teams focused on Y2K, and only on Y2K. Teams were tempted to add other functionality, but leadership made it clear that going off on these tangents was not an option. The result: All products were delivered on schedule and the overall timeline was kept short. The objective was accomplished by the end of 1998 and the customer response was very positive.

# Case Study: The Swiss Stock Exchange Revisited

At the beginning of the chapter, we related the story of the Swiss stock exchange. One of the first steps that Pollyanna took when she started leading the group was to look at what the teams were doing. The overall project's complexity attributes are listed in Table 4.7 and the uncertainty attributes in Table 4.8. The project was clearly a bull, with both high complexity and high uncertainty.

As mentioned earlier, Pollyanna took a different approach working with the server side than she did when working with the client side.

**Table 4.7**   Complexity Attributes

| Attribute | Comments | Score | Graph |
|---|---|---|---|
| Team size | More than 100 | 9 | ■■■■■■■■■ |
| Mission critical | Bet the company | 9 | ■■■■■■■■■ |
| Team location | All in same building; most in the same room | 1 | ■ |
| Team maturity | New team of top talent | 3 | ■■■ |
| Domain gaps | Team knew what the product needed to deliver | 3 | ■■■ |
| Dependencies | Moderate dependencies | 3 | ■■■ |

**Table 4.8**   Uncertainty Attributes

| Attribute | Comments | Score | Graph |
|---|---|---|---|
| Market uncertainty | The market was generally known but new | 3 | ■■■ |
| Technical uncertainty | New technologies | 9 | ■■■■■■■■■ |
| Number of customers | Approximately 50 customers | 3 | ■■■ |
| Project duration | Approximately 2 years | 9 | ■■■■■■■■■ |
| Change | Some change was expected and allowed | 3 | ■■■ |

This case study exemplifies how a bull project can be decomposed into component projects that can then be managed semi-independently. Each of the subprojects for the Swiss stock exchange was run in a different manner, yet coordinated within a structure that supported the overall project.

Tables 4.9 and 4.10 show the complexity and uncertainty attributes of the client and server sides of this project. As you can see from the profile, the server-side project was a cow, whereas the client-side project was a colt. The overall project was still a bull, but each subteam was able to operate in the mode that was best suited for its needs.

Splitting projects into subprojects is a good practice. Many people suggest an ideal subteam size of 5–10 members, and our experience validates this suggestion. In addition to following this guideline, we find it equally important to design project teams at natural boundaries. In the software development world, the design mantra is to partition software such that it has loose coupling and strong cohesion. This mantra is just as applicable to project partitioning. Aim to partition projects in such a manner that they have only loose coupling; in other words, make sure that they are not intricately intertwined with or heavily dependent on other projects. Some dependencies will likely arise, but it is best if the teams can be as independent as possible. Likewise, it is best if there is strong cohesion within the project team. Put simply, we want the subteam working on the same basic aspect of the system.

**Table 4.9**   Complexity Attributes for Server and Client

| Attribute | Server Score | Graph | Client Score | Graph |
|---|---|---|---|---|
| Team size | 9 | ■■■■■■■■■ | 3 | ■■■ |
| Mission critical | 9 | ■■■■■■■■■ | 9 | ■■■■■■■■■ |
| Team location | 1 | ■ | 1 | ■ |
| Team maturity | 3 | ■■■ | 3 | ■■■ |
| Domain gaps | 3 | ■■■ | 3 | ■■■ |
| Dependencies | 3 | ■■■ | 1 | ■ |

**Table 4.10** Uncertainty Attributes for Server and Client

| Attribute | Server Score | Graph | Client Score | Graph |
|-----------|--------------|-------|--------------|-------|
| Market uncertainty | 3 | ■■■ | 9 | ■■■■■■■■■ |
| Technical uncertainty | 3 | ■■■ | 9 | ■■■■■■■■■ |
| Number of customers | 3 | ■■■ | 3 | ■■■ |
| Project duration | 3 | ■■■ | 3 | ■■■ |
| Change | 3 | ■■■ | 9 | ■■■ |

Figure 4.2 shows the partitioning of the client from the server for the Swiss stock exchange and the overall coordination of the full solution.

**FIGURE 4.2** Turning a bull into a cow and a colt

Although some loose coupling was needed from the client team to the server team, most of the focus of the teams' efforts was internal to the needs of the teams' deliverables.

## Using the Assessment to Reduce Risk

Decomposing larger projects into subprojects—the path taken with the Swiss stock exchange—can be a great way to help reduce complexity. In general, any degree of incremental complexity or uncertainty correlates with an incremental risk. Your teams might discover during the assessment that their projects are either more complex or uncertain than necessary to obtain their objective. Sometimes, it is possible to adjust one or more of the project attributes to reduce either complexity or uncertainty and in the process reduce the overall level of risk.

Three approaches can be taken with the risk: reduce it, mitigate it, or accept it. Use the first pass of the assessment to identify any opportunities for reducing or mitigating the risk. This decision making must be balanced by the associated ramifications. Perhaps accepting the risk is preferable if it enables the team to maximize the value potential of the project. Tables 4.11 and 4.12 outline some techniques for reducing or mitigating risk from complexity and uncertainty.

**Table 4.11**   Reducing or Mitigating Complexity Attributes

| Attribute | Ways to Lower the Attribute and Reduce Risk | Process Steps to Mitigate |
|---|---|---|
| Team size | Split teams into smaller cohesive groups. | Make sure teams have shared understanding of their purpose and the overall project success criteria. Bring teams together at regular intervals. Define, communicate, test, and manage project interfaces. |
| Mission critical | Not easy to reduce. | Make critical decisions and overall project status visible to all stakeholders. Ensure that stakeholders understand the consequences of key decisions. |
| Team location | Collocate the team if possible | Bring team members into face-to-face contact often. Invest in high-bandwidth communication and collaboration tools. |

**Table 4.11**   Reducing or Mitigating Complexity Attributes *(continued)*

| Attribute | Ways to Lower the Attribute and Reduce Risk | Process Steps to Mitigate |
|---|---|---|
| Team maturity | Keep experienced teams whole, and leverage them from one release to the next. Integrate new members into the team early. | Make sure that time is allocated for mentoring of new team members, and invest in training and improvement for the entire team. |
| Domain gaps | Staff the team with members who have strong domain knowledge and use them to mentor other team members. Ensure that customer needs are constantly represented. | Educate and expose team members to the domain. Have team members sit with users and experience how they use the product. |
| Dependencies | Eliminate dependencies or work with static versions of dependencies. Build automated tests to check dependencies. | Invest in communication with teams that you are dependent on. Monitor their progress and be clear about your needs. |

**Table 4.12**   Reducing or Mitigating Uncertainty Attributes

| Attribute | Ways to Lower the Attribute and Reduce Risk | Process Steps to Mitigate |
|---|---|---|
| Market uncertainty | Target a specific market segment that is better understood. | Deliver iteratively, utilize prototypes, and elicit customer feedback on a regular basis. |
| Technical uncertainty | Accept proven technologies. Design flexibility into situations to enable decisions to be made in the future. | Delay decisions where the uncertainty will resolve itself. Conduct experiments that will provide information to help resolve the uncertainty. |

*(continues)*

**Table 4.12**   Reducing or Mitigating Uncertainty Attributes  *(continued)*

| Attribute | Ways to Lower the Attribute and Reduce Risk | Process Steps to Mitigate |
|---|---|---|
| Number of customers | Target a specific customer segment or group of customers. | Use a product champion to solicit multiple customer voices and move them in a unified direction. Use the Purpose Alignment Model as a filter. |
| Project duration | Shorten the duration or deliver functionality in incremental releases. | Deliver incrementally and maintain high quality throughout the project. |
| Change | Exert control over change where it has the biggest impact. Delay decisions so that changes can be made without major impact. | Utilize incremental delivery and feedback to enable change to be absorbed into the project. Avoid committing to too much detail early. |

# Product Life Cycle

Products and long-term initiatives tend to have a life cycle that moves through the four quadrants illustrated in Figure 4.3. In our experience, many successful products follow path A: They start with low complexity and moderate uncertainty as skunks, move to greater uncertainty and with a bit more complexity as colts, and then become successful and turn into highly uncertain and highly complex bulls. Over time, the uncertainty dies down and the product becomes a cow. Eventually the complexity is reduced and the project becomes a sheepdog.

Another group of products follow path B and, as a result, never become particularly complex. There's nothing wrong with this route, as these products often end up being profitable, right-sized sheepdogs.

While we have seen numerous attempts to start products on path C, in which the projects are launched directly in the bull quadrant, we have seen very limited success with this approach. Our most successful bull projects have first begun as colts or sheepdogs, then evolved into bulls over time. When a product begins its life cycle as a bull, the combined risk of high complexity and high uncertainty with a new product and a new team is typically just too much to overcome. Certainly there are examples of bull

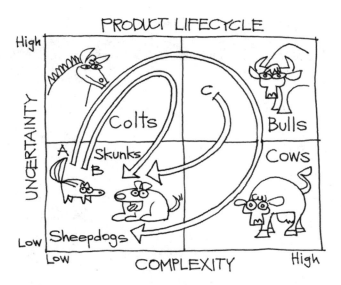

**FIGURE 4.3**    Product life cycle

project teams that have done wonderful things and succeeded, but in our experience they are the exception rather than the rule.

## Case Study: A Lot of Bull

A software company's products had been very successful, but many of its applications were 10 to 20 years old. The development teams had done their best to continually update the application suite, but the architecture was recognized as having limitations. A team of experts was created to embark on a quest to build the next-generation architecture and the initial product solutions. The original idea was to keep the team small, consisting of approximately 15 people.

Within a short time, the team realized the scope of the effort was quite large. Rather than reduce the scope to match the capacity of the smaller team, the decision was made to increase the team size to approximately 50 people.

The overall project's complexity attributes are listed in Table 4.13 and the uncertainty attributes in Table 4.14. The project is clearly in the bull category, with both high complexity and high uncertainty.

**Table 4.13** Complexity Attributes for Next Generation

| Attribute | Comments | Score | Graph |
|---|---|---|---|
| Team size | More than 50 | 9 | ■■■■■■■■■ |
| Mission critical | New product | 3 | ■■■ |
| Team location | Distributed in Houston, Austin, and Denver | 9 | ■■■■■■■■■ |
| Team maturity | New team of experts | 3 | ■■■ |
| Domain gaps | Not all developers are domain experts | 3 | ■■■ |
| Dependencies | Major dependencies | 9 | ■■■■■■■■■ |

**Table 4.14** Uncertainty Attributes for Next Generation

| Attribute | Comments | Score | Graph |
|---|---|---|---|
| Market uncertainty | Brand-new market space | 9 | ■■■■■■■■■ |
| Technical uncertainty | Brand-new technology | 9 | ■■■■■■■■■ |
| Number of customers | New solution for the market | 3 | ■■■ |
| Project duration | Approximately 12 months | 9 | ■■■ |
| Change | Embrace and/or create change | 9 | ■■■■■■■■■ |

## What the Leaders Did

The project demonstrated some interesting dynamics. The developers had just read about Extreme Programming and wanted to try out some of the ideas; they knew there was a lot of uncertainty, so they wanted to run the project like a colt. The project managers had just seen the success of a well-run cow project, and, recognizing the complexity of this project, they wanted to run the project like a cow. Not surprisingly, the differing perspectives created some significant tension on the team. The project floundered for quite some time. It took a few iterations, but fortunately the team ultimately recognized that the project really was a bull and needed to be treated as such. Once they came to that realization, the project managers understood the need to be able to adapt to the uncertainty, and the developers realized the need to have structured communications and better documentation to deal with the complexity. In retrospect, it probably would have been wiser to stick with the original plan to start with a small team and let the project evolve over time from a colt to a bull.

## Iterative and Incremental Delivery

One key aspect of project management that is highlighted by this case study is the importance of iterative delivery and adaptation to cope with high uncertainty. This project was charged with delivering new products—yet no one knew exactly what the market needed. Iterative development was critical so that the team members could see working versions of the software, thereby enabling them to make adjustments and drive the product in the direction needed for the market. Likewise, it was important for team members to be able to reflect on the development process and discover what was working and what was not working. In this case, the team came to the realization that changes to their process would be necessary if they wanted to be successful.

# Leadership Development

As noted earlier in this chapter, the skills necessary to lead a bull project are quite different from the skills necessary to lead a sheepdog project.

Bull projects require leaders who can coordinate large teams and can navigate through the uncertainty minefield. Sometimes sheepdog projects can be simple enough that they require very little direct leadership. This way of looking at projects and the associated leadership styles required provides a basic tool for leadership development. Leaders exhibit excellence in four primary skill areas, as depicted in Figure 4.4:

- People: The ability to coordinate and lead people.
- Business: Connecting to and comprehending the business drivers.
- Process: Understanding the appropriate processes to get the job done.
- Technology: Understanding the technology used to develop the solutions.

As shown in Figure 4.5, the key leadership skills required to move from a sheepdog to a colt lie in the areas of business and technology. Why? Because the uncertainty is either in the marketplace or in the technology. As such, the leader of a colt project needs to have a good connection to the source of the uncertainty. Likewise, to move from a sheepdog to a cow requires skills in the areas of working with people and processes. The larger teams and the overall coordination associated with following such a path require a leader who can work well with people and utilize appropriate processes to facilitate the overall project coordination. To be capable of running a bull project, a project leader needs to have core skills in all

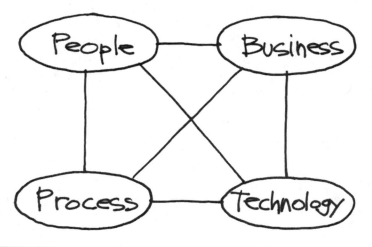

**FIGURE 4.4**   Skill areas exhibited by project leaders

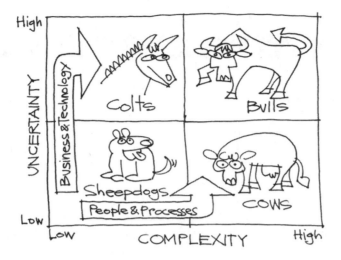

**FIGURE 4.5**  Project profile

four areas. The leader doesn't need to be an expert in the technology or in the business, but does need to understand it well enough that he or she can comprehend the consequences of making and guiding decisions in these areas.

The five-stage Dreyfus model [1] is commonly used for assessing skill acquisition and competencies. Many people find it convenient to simplify this to a three-level progression from novice to practitioner to master. In the latter model, the three levels map to the actions of read, write, and delete. A novice can read rules and generally follow the procedures, but isn't proficient enough to be able to write rules. A solid practitioner is capable of writing rules for others to follow, but is generally still following standard procedures himself or herself. By comparison, someone who has reached the mastery level knows just which rules he or she needs to follow and which rules can be deleted.

Table 4.15 shows the base levels of competencies required by project quadrant. A leader of a sheepdog project must have core capabilities in all areas but need not excel in any. As previously mentioned, a leader of a colt project must be strong in the areas of business and technology. To lead a cow project, the leader must be strong in the areas of people and process. A leader of a bull project needs to be strong across all four areas and must have particularly strong skills in working with people. These leaders need

**Table 4.15**   Competencies Required by Project Quadrant

|  | People | Process | Technology | Business |
|---|---|---|---|---|
| Sheepdog | Novice | Novice | Novice | Novice |
| Colt | Novice | Novice | Practitioner | Practitioner |
| Cow | Practitioner | Practitioner | Novice | Novice |
| Bull | Master | Practitioner | Practitioner | Practitioner |

to have mastery in working with people and be able to break down the traditional rules on occasion to get things done.

It is important to match the appropriate leadership style and capability to the project needs. The leadership skills required to deal with uncertainty are not the same as those required to manage complexity. Some leaders are naturally drawn to managing uncertainty, whereas others are naturally drawn to managing complexity. For bull projects, a comprehensive set of skills is required to be able to manage both complexity and uncertainty. Some leaders who are naturally drawn to one dimension may find it difficult to cross over to the other dimension. Those who wish to develop their leadership potential will look to develop their skills by taking on more diverse challenges.

Some people can make the jump directly from leading a colt or cow project to leading a bull project. For others, it is advantageous to develop experience with a cow project before becoming a leader of a colt project, and vice versa. Leaders of sheepdogs can advance their leadership experience by taking on colts or cows or by taking on progressively more challenging sheepdogs.

## Portfolio Assessment

An assessment of certainty and complexity can also provide useful information when looking at an overall portfolio of projects. The most critical consideration is that the organization should not try to take on more projects in any particular quadrant than it has capable leaders for those projects. This constraint is particularly applicable for bull projects. An organization is unlikely to have a large number of project leaders who are capable of delivering on bull projects.

A typical portfolio will consist of projects that are distributed throughout the four quadrants of the Context Leadership Model (as shown in Figure 4.6). In the example shown in Figure 4.6, a high percentage of projects is in the sheepdog category. Obviously, a younger or very established organization might have a project distribution that skews in one direction or another. The important thing is to make sure that, whatever the distribution is, the organization understands the reasons for that distribution and then builds the organizational capacity to make those projects happen.

**FIGURE 4.6**  Sample portfolio of the Context Leadership Model

## Summary

Figure 4.7 provides an overall summary of the Context Leadership Model. While all projects are not created equal, an examination of the complexity and uncertainty characteristics of projects is likely to reveal groupings of projects that behave similarly. Using this model can provide guidance for leaders to help with running projects and overall project portfolios. The complexity and uncertainty assessment can be used to better understand some portions of a project's risk profile and to look for opportunities to reduce some of that risk. The model also can play a role in leadership

**FIGURE 4.7**   Context Leadership Model summary

development. The skills needed to manage uncertainty are different from those necessary to manage complexity. Aligning and developing leadership skills to be compatible with the project portfolio can significantly affect project success.

# References

[1] Dreyfus, Stuart, and Dreyfus, Hubert. *A Five-Stage Model of the Mental Activities Involved in Directed Skill Acquisition*. Berkeley, CA: University of California Operation Research Center, February 1980.

# CHAPTER 5

# DECISIONS

## The Big Ideas

- Business decisions focus on delivering value to the organization and to the marketplace. Life is much better if everyone in the organization understands what generates value and makes decisions that improve value.
- You can develop a value model that helps you make better decisions, but this model is not just a calculation that generates a numerical value. Instead, it is a conversation that you should revisit often, especially when conditions change.

## What Do We Do? When Do We Do It?

This just might be one of the hardest project decisions you have ever had to make. The vice president of operations is convinced that she needs a new warehouse management system (WMS) and she has the cost–benefit analysis to prove it. But you have reservations. Over the years, you have upgraded the legacy WMS to include functionality the VP of operations was convinced would generate value. To date, none of the upgrade projects has yielded anything close to the expected results. The VP of operations blames the legacy system for the previous failings and believes that an entirely new system will be the clean slate that will finally produce the estimated improvement. To grease the skids, she has petitioned you to support this project at the upcoming steering committee meeting.

You and the VP of operations have worked closely on many projects, and you have built a strong relationship. But now you are torn—you have too many questions. Could the distribution center personnel achieve the expected benefits if they were simply willing to change their work processes and business rules? Does the staff have the capability to learn the new system well enough to generate results? How good does the distribution center need to be? Is the current performance good enough? Why does the company need to make this decision now? What happens if you don't replace the WMS? And for you personally, how can you factor your questions into the decision-making process so that the company makes the right decision and do so in a way that protects your relationship with the VP of operations?

If you are like the rest of us, you find it extremely difficult to make such decisions in a consistent way. And, if you do find a process that works well for making one decision, it might not work equally effectively for another one. The challenge just grows when you factor in the demands of today's dynamic and rapid marketplace. What used to work just doesn't seem to do so anymore.

You need a way to do the right things the right way. To do the right things the right way, you need to build a value model. This model helps you answer three critical questions:

- What do we do?
- When do we do it?
- Should we continue doing it?

Even better, value models help you make decisions that deliver real value to your organization.

## Challenges and Solutions

Without value models, you risk deciding in favor of something that does not generate business value or deciding against something that does. For example, an Internet-based company was investigating new growth opportunities. A marketing analyst identified that various parts of the former Soviet Union, specifically the Ukraine, represented huge opportunities for growth. There was one tiny little problem: Ukrainians typically did not use, and did not even own, credit cards. If the company wanted to market its products to people in the Ukraine, it would have to provide a means for people to pay other than by credit card.

The development team members were up to their necks in work for the new version of the product, but the head of marketing was adamant that they should at least figure out how much it would cost to develop an alternative payment mechanism for people living in Ukraine. The development team agreed to estimate the cost, figuring it would be good information to have when making a decision about whether to move forward with the new functionality. Their estimate: $50,000.

In the meantime, the marketing department determined that the company's revenue stream would increase by $10,000 per month as a result of opening the Ukrainian market. With the company's 50% profit margin, this analysis produced a payback period of 10 months—far less than the 1-year payback threshold. However, with the backlog in development, 10 months was deemed not good enough. The head of marketing had his analyst sharpen her pencil and revise the estimate. A week later, the analysis miraculously showed that the Ukrainian market would generate $20,000 in revenue per month and the payback period was 5 months. This venture was now the best project in the portfolio.

A couple of months later, the functionality was completed, tested, and released into production under budget. That was six months ago. As of this writing, the average incremental revenue generated by the project is a less than thrilling $700 per month.

Many of us try to put some structure around our decision-making process. The most common approach is to put the costs and the benefits through some type of calculation, which then spits out a number. Nevertheless, this approach often fails because decision makers place too much emphasis on cost and benefit information that is difficult to determine, particularly when talking about the future. Organizations love to focus on improving their cost estimation processes, but the results are always subject to the same constraint—these processes always produce an estimate, and estimates are often wrong. In the software industry, repeated studies have shown that cost estimates are often off by a factor of 2 or even 4. The quantification of benefits in many organizations is a complete black art. If costs are an estimate, then the quantification of benefits is often a wild guess. These cost–benefit calculations give a precise, but inaccurate value number. Yet these numbers are held in high esteem because they are set in concrete and, therefore, should drive logical decision making. Of course, over time people learn the system, and because these calculations are based on several assumptions, the system is easily gamed to meet some established decision criteria.

Value models provide a clear advantage over the traditional decision-making models. Value models include a number of factors and are based on delivering value to the marketplace, thereby making the organization better in a meaningful way.

In this chapter, we build a complete, generic value model one step at a time. You can then use this approach to make the big decisions you face.

You can build value models for decisions ranging from acquisitions to functionality design. Just keep in mind that the output of a value model will likely not be a number or a calculation. Instead, the model results are a manifestation of the various factors that go into making a better decision. Better decisions are a conversation, not a number.

To build value models, we start with the purpose, so that we understand if the decision is intended to differentiate the organization in the marketplace or to help it achieve and maintain parity. We then add the array of things we need to consider when making the decision—complexity and uncertainty, market window, team and product maturity, and a different way of thinking about cost–benefit analysis. Next, we examine the timing of decisions. You may be surprised to learn that you don't always have to decide right now. Finally, we take a look at how you act on those decisions. As you might expect, all of this activity occurs in a collaborative environment. Collaborating on purpose, considerations, costs and benefits, and the value model is the right way to do the right things.

## Building a Value Model

Identifying the inputs to the value model provides the framework for the conversations necessary to improve your decision making. As shown in Figure 5.1, there are three types of inputs:

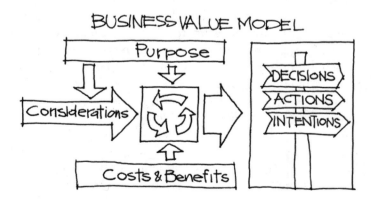

**Figure 5.1**  Business value model

- Purpose
- Considerations
- Costs and benefits

## Value Model Inputs: Purpose

One of the first questions you should ask is, "Why do this?" In other words, what is the purpose? Will your decision lead to more market share? Will it help you win new customers? Or is the purpose of this decision to help you maintain your customers and market position? The value that your decision generates is based partially on how well you align your decision with the purpose. If you need to close a gap in one of your mission-critical activities, your decision should not attempt to create differentiation. If you need to use an activity to grow market share and gain new customers, your decision should not be satisfied with reaching parity. This comes from the Purpose Alignment Model described in Chapter 2.

For example, one company was deciding whether to proceed with an acquisition. This company had completed its initial due diligence and, with some minor exceptions, believed that the acquisition was the right thing to do. When making the decision, the CEO of the company asked his version of the purpose question: "If we complete this acquisition, will it make us a better company or will this acquisition position us to maintain our current market leadership?" As a group, the management team agreed that this takeover was a defensive acquisition. This understanding did not change the company's decision to proceed with the acquisition. Instead, it changed how the company proceeded with the acquisition. It designed the acquisition to fulfill its defensive, parity purpose. Recognizing the purpose of this decision also helped the company realize that, if it could not finalize the acquisition on its terms, it could walk away from the transaction and find other ways to defend its market position.

As another example, the director of Internet marketing was deciding how to design a community for her company's customers. The company's claim to fame was how it converged commerce and community, and the design of this social network was intended to help the company maintain its differentiation edge. The director treated the decision accordingly by setting the following decision goals: market leadership in product reviews, filters to help customers find the right equipment for the right use, and community-provided support.

In another case, the vice president of manufacturing had to decide which type of equipment to purchase for the expansion of a manufacturing line. As he sorted through the options, he realized that his decision should be partially based on the purpose of the expansion. While the expansion was needed to meet existing customer demand, the actual equipment was used in the manufacturing line to support—not create—sustainable competitive advantage. Recognizing this fact, the VP revised his equipment decision criteria to include how broadly the equipment was used in the marketplace; thus the equipment decision supported the best practices associated with parity processes. In addition, the VP eliminated an earlier criterion that the equipment be highly customizable to enable every imaginable process design. While the equipment needed to be flexible, it did not need to be unique.

With purpose being one of the inputs to the improved decision-making process, how do you determine the purpose of your decision? One technique that works to identify and frame the purpose is to use the collaboration process described in Chapter 3. Ask those persons who are making the decision to answer the following questions:

- What's the problem?
- Who does it affect?
- What's the impact?
- What's a successful solution?

Or ask them to answer this set of questions:

- Who do you serve, and what do they want and need most?
- What do you provide to help them?
- What is the best way to provide this?
- How do you know you are succeeding?

Have the group compile the answers to those questions into a single statement. The statement itself is helpful, but what is more useful is the conversation that goes into creating it. During that conversation, identify the various assumptions, risks, and constraints—things that are worth noticing because they could affect the value delivered by the idea or the project.

Once you understand how your organization defines "differentiating" activities, sort out the purpose of your decision. Answering the following questions may help you align your decision with purpose:

- Will this activity help increase market share? (In other words, is it a differentiating activity?)
- Do you need to do this activity to hold on to your market share? (Is it a parity decision? Remember that many of your activities have a

parity orientation, so many of your decisions will be aimed at achieving and maintaining parity.)

- Will this activity generate a sustainable competitive advantage?

If you think your decision has a differentiating purpose, test it by asking a familiar question: Would you put this message on a billboard to advertise your company? One project team initially believed that a decision to put "an animated feature on their Web site" fell into the differentiating category until we asked, "Do you want your billboard to say, 'Buy from us because we have the best animated presentation on our Web site?'" The decision makers then quickly moved the issue to the parity category and made the decision accordingly.

## Value Model Inputs: Considerations

Understanding the purpose is a giant step, but it's not enough. When making a decision, what other things should you take into consideration? In addition to purpose, and beyond costs and benefits, are there other considerations—impossible- or hard-to-quantify factors you should include in your decision-making conversations? For example, will an initiative improve your product, service delivery, or organizational flexibility? This consideration is difficult to quantify, but may be incredibly important in your value decision.

Bring the stakeholders together and use the collaboration process (see Chapter 3) to brainstorm all the considerations in relationship to the decision or decisions you are making. Keep in mind the purpose that you have agreed to as part of the value model (discussed in the previous section). A differentiating activity will have different decision considerations than a parity activity.

Let's look at some examples of considerations that you may want to include as input in your value model.

### Meeting a Market Window

Does the value delivered by a product or service change if you miss a market window? What about process changes? Is there a difference in value that you should factor into your decisions if the initiative supports a required deadline? Do you have the resources needed to deliver a successful outcome in the time frame given? For example, Christmas tradeshows occur midyear, and delivery to retail stores must occur several months before the holiday. What happens to the value in terms of revenues, customer satisfaction, and loyalty if you miss both deadlines? Similar situations hold when conferences and major sporting events are considerations and their hard dates cannot be moved. Other considerations could be whether you need to hit the market window on the front or back end.

One valuable exercise is to have the team members draw out their view of how the market window behaves; Figure 5.2 shows an example. Very time-sensitive markets follow curve A in Figure 5.2, while less sensitive markets behave like curve C. Simply having the team come to an understanding of the market window dynamics will substantially inform their decision process.

### Uncertainty in the Marketplace

How much uncertainty is there in your decision? How can you factor the unknown into your value model? For one company, there were hints that new regulations would soon be announced but the actual form of the regulations was unclear. In this case, the organization's value model included a number of decision branches linked to the various potential forms of the regulations. Each branch mapped out the impact of the regulation on the business and how the company could exploit the regulation in the marketplace. As soon as project team members saw solid evidence of one of the regulation paths, they knew which branch to use. In this way, considering uncertainty improved their decision making.

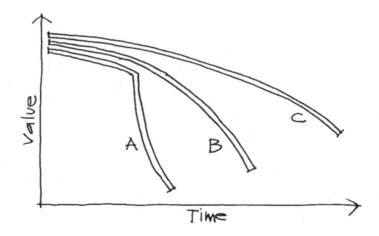

**Figure 5.2** Market window

### Knowledge of Your Product Team

What about the knowledge of your product team? Your marketing team? In periods of transitioning technology (i.e., mainframe to personal computers, stand-alone applications to the Internet), your teams may be undergoing a transition as well. How will this evolution affect your value model? Tools that can assist in this area include the Context Leadership Model described in Chapter 4 and the associated leadership table.

Recently, one of our clients realized he needed to upgrade his company's IT infrastructure. The legacy database and operating systems were no longer supported, and the client questioned whether they could support the company's transaction volumes. As we worked with him on the considerations to use in his value model, it occurred to him that he had to factor into the decision his team's lack of knowledge about the current versions of the database and operating system. This consideration helped the client decide that he needed a predecessor to his database and operating system decision. He first needed to train his staff on the more recent versions of the technology. Without this predecessor step, his upgrade decision would likely be wasted.

### What if You Don't Do This?

Another important consideration is what happens if you decide not to go forward with the idea. What will happen to your company? Perhaps the more important questions to consider are these: Do we need to be in this market at all? If we *are* going to be in the market, do we need to be first in the marketplace? Will we lose market share if we don't follow through on this initiative?

One industrial equipment manufacturer considered what would happen if it was not the first to market with a new technology. The value model the team members built was based on the consideration that the company's primary competitor would struggle with the new technology and allow the company to "go to school" on the competitor's mistakes. They prepared internally to mobilize the entire organization to utilize the new technology once it was released by the competitor. Their decision consideration proved correct: The competition botched the new technology, and this company quickly applied the lessons learned to ensure its own successful launch.

In another example, a health services company recognized that its patient access portal was well behind that of its competitors'. For this organization, the consideration was that if it did implement a parity patient portal, it would fall further behind.

### What Expectations Have You Set?

Often one of the biggest considerations when making a decision has to do with expectation management. If you don't meet the expectations that you have set, what will be the consequences? Apple released the iPhone in 2007 inside the window to which the company had committed. This first version was not the complete product, however, and Apple released news that another version was in the works at the same time it launched the first version. Why? One reason may have been to meet the company's commitment to the marketplace so it could maintain customer loyalty. What do you think would have been the consequences if Apple had not delivered on the agreed-upon date?

### Do You Need to Mitigate Risks?

What risks and pitfalls do you see? In general, it is difficult to calculate the costs associated with risks. Doing so effectively requires certainty about the probability of future events. In building value models, we can consider risk without having to quantify risks. In some circumstances, it is even possible to reduce uncertainty by implementing interim decisions sooner that help you gather more information.

For example, suppose the warranty period for your hardware is about to end. How risky is it to not replace the hardware? This risk might be difficult to quantify but is an important consideration. How quickly could you replace the hardware in the event of a failure? How does this lag time affect your risks? In what other ways might you mitigate the risks of hardware failure? Extend the warranty? Do more frequent backups? Considering risk mitigation opens up your choices and helps you better frame your decisions.

### Do You Need More Information?

Do you need more information? Should you wait? Why should you wait?

We needed to define our Sarbanes-Oxley Act (SOX) compliance project plan. The board of directors expected us to make a presentation identifying the expected level of effort so that they could review and approve the annual audit fee proposal. At the time, the Public Company Accounting Oversight Board (PCAOB)—the body that defines the standards for SOX compliance—was still debating changes in the latest version of the SOX standard. To make the right decision, we needed to wait until after the board meeting to define our project plan. Otherwise, we risked over-staffing our internal and external project teams and spending too much on our SOX compliance.

Considering our need for better information, we broke our compliance project into two phases. The first phase included the work that we knew we would have to do, independent of the PCAOB's decision. The second phase included the work that could change when the PCAOB released its new standard. Working with the board of directors, we had our auditors scope out the work for the first phase and start that work while we and they waited for PCAOB clarity.

### *Political Considerations*

Sometimes, we need to consider the politics of our decisions. For example, do we have the executive buy-in we need to move forward? If not, how does that lack of support affect our decision? Do different functions have different expectations and goals for the project or decision? How easily can we get them to resolve these differences in a way that does not limit our success? When making a decision, we don't need to have all of the answers to these questions, but we do need to consider the impact these questions have on the decision-making process.

## Value Model Inputs: Costs and Benefits

The result of the cost–benefit analysis remains an important input to your value model—but it is not the sole input to your decision-making process. In some cases, costs and benefits will inform your decision. In other cases, they will not.

For example, a municipality was making a decision about replacing its legacy telephone system with a voice-over-IP (VOIP) system. As the CIO gathered information about the costs and benefits, she quickly realized that the $2 million in annual savings was the most important factor in deciding what to do. Other factors, such as user training and familiarity and staff knowledge, became implementation considerations, not decision considerations.

Clearly, cost–benefit analysis still has its place. However, it should be used in decision making in conjunction with other factors, including the purpose of the initiative and the host of considerations that influence the value produced by the initiative.

With cost–benefit analysis being part of the answer, do we really have to put so much work into creating these analyses? No. Cost–benefit analysis results are useful in support of decisions. As long as two initiatives or ideas are estimated with the same level of precision, better decisions can be made. Thus, instead of spending a great deal of time trying to establish estimates at a precision level that may not be attainable, you should seek to establish relative measures of cost, benefit, and value and then converge on more precise, financially based measures as you gather more information throughout the course of project implementation.

## Using Value Models to Make Better Decisions

The inputs to value models include purpose, considerations, and costs and benefits. But how do you use these inputs in practice to make better decisions that generate real value for your organization? How can you use value models when someone asks you for an NPV or ROI number and all you have is a model?

# It's a Conversation, Not a Number

Have you ever made a decision, implemented the decision, and then been confronted with a raft of questions: "What were you thinking?", "Why did you do that?", or "Why did you do it that way?" How can you avoid this disconnect? Bring the stakeholders together and build the value model as a team. Agree to the purpose and brainstorm the considerations. Put the considerations in priority order. Have the team discuss the costs and benefits. Don't look for *one* number.

The bigger the decision, the more likely that people will view and value the purpose, considerations, and associated costs and benefits differently. Listen to the conversation as you build the model. Do you have major discrepancies in how people think? Does marketing feel one idea or initiative has high value, while finance thinks just the opposite? Expand the conversation to understand the differences and the thinking that brought people to their conclusions.

As you sort through the discrepancies, look for common ground in your conversations, particularly in regard to the critical decision points:

- What do we do?
- When do we do it?
- Should we continue doing it?

Let's look at each of these questions with some examples.

## What Do We Do?

In one company that designs and builds the hinges in technical arms for space vehicles, it takes one year from design of the product to its delivery to the market. To facilitate meeting market demands that might arise near the end of the delivery cycle, the company adds "hooks" into the product that support "possible features" that customers may want in the future. Marketing and engineering personnel meet regularly to decide which "hooks" to build using value models. They also use value models to decide when to use the hooks during the delivery stage. Their value models think ahead to what the company might need to do so that team members are prepared for future iterations. For this company, flexibility is what to do.

## When Do We Do It?

When your stakeholders say, "We have to do this right now!" ask, "Why?" Understanding their urgency is part of the value model.

The most difficult question to answer is "What not to do?" or, more simply put, "What can we delay?" The longer you can delay a decision, the more information you might have. Of course, you also risk missing your market window or deadline if you delay too long. Look at the uncertainty considerations in your value model. Do you have many of them, such as market uncertainty, domain knowledge uncertainty, or experience uncertainty? To resolve some of these uncertainties, you may need to implement partial ideas to gather information. But do not wait too long; find the right balance for your company.

Remember that delaying the implementation of an idea does not mean that you will *never* do it. Well, that might be the case—but a delay really just means you will decide later.

## Should We Continue Doing This?

One of the hardest decisions you will ever have to make is to stop doing something that is already under way. There are several reasons why you should stop an initiative. The most desirable reason is that you have accomplished what you set out to do: The initiative has met its purpose, delivered the expected return, and met the constraints of the considerations. To know when you have reached this point, however, you have to know what "done" looks like. This point may seem obvious, but we have seen far too many cases where organizations dove into an initiative or project without a clear understanding of what successful completion would look like. (How many "mission accomplished" parties have you held for projects that just kept going?) This point also highlights a critical benefit of building and using a value model. The model describes the purpose, considerations, and desired return. Thus the value model also establishes the backstop for deciding—Look, another decision!—what "done" is.

Value models also help you recognize when you should change your mind because a decision is causing you to head in the wrong direction. This situation can arise when the purpose of the decision changes, the considerations change, or the costs and benefits change. Using the value model as a baseline, the wrong direction is easier to identify.

Later in this chapter we discuss delivering results in chunks. This helpful strategy allows you to revisit your project decisions with the most current information and have confidence in the decision to stop work on a project and still know that you have delivered some value.

## Do We Have to Decide This Today?

Before you jump into making all your decisions, ask the following questions: Which decisions can you delay? What is driving you to make the decision today? If you keep insisting that you must make a decision now, why? Sometimes projects or ideas stall while you are trying to figure out something or decide something that can actually wait. You can get more information if you wait when you don't have enough now. Things will change in the marketplace. A critical issue may become a non-issue.

Most people dislike uncertainty. They would rather take the risk of making a wrong decision now than live with the uncertainty for as long as necessary to improve their chances of making the right decision later.

Instead of making a decision right away with limited information, determine when that decision needs to be made, in terms of either time or the conditions that need to be met. Deferring the decision does not give you a free pass, however. In the intervening time, collect and investigate information that improves your chances of making the right decision.

Remember that deferring a decision does not provide you with an open-ended time frame. Instead of saying, "Not yet," you are really saying, "Make the decision when . . ." This approach gives you certainty over when the decision will be made and makes you more comfortable with delaying the decision. By revisiting your value model often, you will come to this decision again and again, yet make it only when you really need to.

A medical software company wanted to provide doctors with an electronic medical record (EMR) system, which patients could also use to view their records and get test results online. The project stalled over an internal debate about whether the EMR system should include the results of critical tests such as cancer screenings. One faction felt that such information should be delivered in person by a doctor. The other faction felt that patients would want to know the information as soon as possible rather than wait for an appointment. While the debate raged, the work stopped. Should the team support business rules to provide potentially bad news? If not, how should the EMR communicate that the patient information was available only in person or on the phone? The company's response to this dilemma was to postpone this one decision. The team could build an EMR system that delivered test results but excluded the delivery of bad news until after the EMR system was deployed. That way, the decision could be based on customer preference.

The idea of deferring a decision sounds great, but how do you avoid analysis paralysis—the act of always gathering information but never making a decision? How do you determine the appropriate time to decide? It depends on the nature of the decision. You want to make the decision at a point where you can gather as much information as possible, still have time to act on that information, and yet not incur so much cost from delay that the value you realize is seriously degraded. This point is time is called the last responsible moment.

To determine the last responsible moment, consider the pace of change in your environment and your desire and ability to react to that change. If conditions in your environment change frequently but you are able to quickly respond to those changes, delay your decisions until as late as possible so that you can incorporate the most up-to-date conditions. This time frame will depend on your ability to respond to the change, the cost of doing so, and the time required for you to react.

On some occasions, further delay would be irresponsible, yet you may not be entirely comfortable with the amount of uncertainty. The reality is that because delaying the decision would be irresponsible, it will be necessary to bite the bullet and proceed based on the best information available. Sometimes in these situations it may be possible to make a decision that leaves future options open as more clarity becomes available.

# Deliver in Chunks to Embrace Change in the Marketplace

Too many times, organizations determine the value of an idea or project, make a decision, and wait until the end of the project to see if they have enough value to go to market with the result. On other occasions, their go/no-go decisions are made with old or insufficient information. Making decisions is not easy in a changing environment. You are trying to deliver to a marketplace where the needs and wants of your target customers are constantly changing, where your competition wants to deliver value faster than you, and where you need to reduce costs while increasing productivity and quality.

The inputs to the value model are not fixed. As time marches on, the inputs will change: Your market window might shift (most likely, shorten or grow smaller), your competition might beat you to market so that your differentiating product is now a parity product. Indeed, any number of things could change during the execution of your carefully crafted plan. And don't forget that throughout the entire process, you are continuously learning more about the market and your organization's environment. How, then, can you structure your value model to take advantage of these changing inputs?

After you have built the value model, decided what to do, and determined in what order to do those things, divide the activities into groups based on their value (taken from the value model). Select "chunks" of activities and deliver them iteratively and incrementally as described in Chapter 4. Take the (relatively) highest-valued features/projects/ideas (a "chunk") and start building them. Don't let the time to implement the decision stretch out for too long; one to three months at most is the limit. In rapidly changing environments, this span could even be as short as two weeks.

At the end of each "chunk," take a look at how much value has been generated using the value model—not the same one you used to make the initial decisions, but rather the value model that now includes any changes in purpose, considerations, and costs and benefits—and make a new set of decisions. The value model is forward looking, so sunk costs that have already been expended should not enter into the model. The real question is "Going forward, what is the best thing to do now?"

By building and using the revised value model, you will have improved the quality of some of your inputs. You will know more about the costs and the benefits. You will know more about the validity and scope of the considerations. You might now be in a position to say that you have delivered enough value and are "done." You might also be in a position to recognize that you will never deliver enough value, so it is time to stop and select a different path. Thus we see the value in using the value model to match decision points to the model inputs.

As we implement each "chunk" we revisit and possibly revise the value model as shown in Figure 5.3., for making our next set of decisions and defining the next "chunk." For each "chunk" of delivery, ask the following questions:

- Is there anything you need to learn before you need to make your next go/no-go decision? Consider including activities specifically designed to learn what you need to know to improve your decision making.
- How can you improve the way in which you measure value? After considering the investment costs, add activities that can help you improve how you measure the value model inputs.

Now you can add activities to the "chunk" cycle to assist you in making the next round of decisions. Let's look at an example.

Adding data to a data warehouse to support operational reporting is always a difficult decision. You want to know how much data to add, what it will cost, and whether it will deliver any real value. When will you know? Using the value model, focus the conversation on which data might

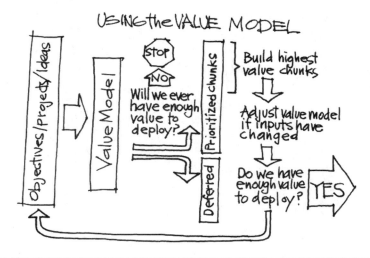

**FIGURE 5.3**    Revisiting the value model

contribute the most value to your internal users and/or your customers. Then, add a chunk of the data and see which benefits appear.

For example, at a health insurance company, a development team needed to add data to a data warehouse to aid with the measurement of the claims processing performance. The team members were given a budget that was too small to deliver all the data they needed. They had to find a way to deliver something within the approved budget that provided enough information to make a noticeable difference in their claims processing performance, and also justified the investment so that requesting additional funding to deliver the remaining functionality would be easier.

The team members decided to focus on 4 of 20 performance metrics. They were able to deliver functionality that helped the operational area improve its performance metric scores by 15% and reduce claims inventory by a factor of 10. These results made it easy to justify the delivery of the other 16 performance measures in two more chunks, improving performance and claims inventory even further.

## Case Study: Improved Customer Retention

Let's now look at an example of how one company built a value model and discovered that it had all the time it needed to make good decisions.

The chief marketing officer (CMO) at the company had a vague, yet interesting idea for how to improve customer retention. He had developed a theory about customer life-cycle management. This theory assumed that once customers first did business with the company, the company could, through the correct customer analysis and promotions, build a lifetime customer relationship. This idea required fairly significant changes to the customer relationship management (CRM) and marketing campaign management systems. The organization needed to create new customer tiers in its CRM system and do marketing promotion experiments to assign customers to an initial tier. Once a customer was placed in the assigned tier, the company would use different promotions to move the customer to a higher tier.

To gauge the company's appetite for such a project, the CMO pitched the concept to the IT executive steering committee. The chief financial officer (CFO) immediately veered into the cost–benefit analysis for this project. He wanted to know the numbers for the expected project benefits. After all, the company's leaders needed to know both the costs and the benefits before they could determine whether this project merited approval through their portfolio management process.

As the CMO sat down to plan how to approach the cost–benefit analysis, it occurred to him that this project was a perfect candidate for a model, not a number. While he could be somewhat accurate in defining the costs to revise the CRM and campaign management systems, the benefits were nebulous and, therefore, difficult to determine. The basis for this customer retention program was that a financial benefit was derived from improved customer retention. But what was that value? The CMO had no idea as to the lifetime value of a customer. He could run a series of reports that would show how much money, on average, a customer spent each year, but there was no way of tracking how many years a customer remained a customer.

How many customers purchased one time and then never again? How could the company link purchases with customers? If the CMO hoped to define some number as the lifetime value of a retained customer, it quickly became apparent that a randomly generated number would be as accurate as the number that any such analysis would generate. Clearly, the company could not rely on cost–benefit analysis to make a go/no-go project decision.

Armed with this understanding, the CMO started over. He expanded his decision-making process to include purpose and considerations. First, what was the purpose of this project? If the company was successful in appropriately managing the relationship with its customers, the ensuing customer loyalty would add to its sustainable competitive advantage. The project fell into the differentiating category.

Second, besides costs and benefits, what else should the CMO consider? There were certainly benefits to consider. For example, if the company did not do this project, how else could it improve its customer retention rate and per-customer sales volume? One of the company's strategic initiatives was to first understand and then anticipate market trends. Were there elements of this project that supported this initiative? Even though the long-term benefits were difficult to quantify, could the project provide any shorter-term benefits?

As the CMO thought through these considerations, he realized the need to approach this project in "chunks." For example, to specify the lifetime value of a customer, the company needed to first link customers to sales transactions. This meant some type of customer identification program. To effectively manage a lifetime relationship, the company needed to better understand customers' reasons for doing business with the company.

Linking customers to sales transactions and understanding purchase motivation became the first two "chunks." Each chunk would deliver business value and benefits; in addition, it would fill in knowledge gaps about the lifetime value of a retained customer.

To link customers to transactions, the CMO proposed a customer loyalty program. Because the actual purpose of the loyalty program was to achieve parity, the CMO proposed a standard—rather than unique—loyalty program. Treating the loyalty program as a parity initiative allowed the CMO to piggyback on the experience of others to quantify the costs and benefits of the program.

The CMO used a different decision design when it came to determining purchase motivation. He believed that if the company could really understand the primary driver behind purchase decisions, this factor would provide strong differentiation. To unearth relevant data, the CMO proposed an extensive customer survey and segmentation study. Armed with this information, the company could better target its marketing and advertising. This would, in turn, generate immediate financial benefits and ideally increase per-customer sales over the long term.

The CMO returned to the IT steering committee with the value model approach. The company did not need to launch the big, expensive project with "vague" benefits, he said. Instead, the long-term plan was now to use the right triggers at the right times to manage the lifetime relationship with customers. Each chunk had its own purpose, considerations, costs, and benefits. Each chunk would also provide evidence as to whether it was worth proceeding to the next chunk. That next chunk would map events in customers' lives so that the company could, depending on the customer segment, respond with the right products for the right events (now that sounds like something with nebulous benefits).

The steering committee loved the approach. In place of a big project with big uncertainty, they got concise, meaningful projects that funded themselves. They could defer decisions about events in customers' lives and both learn and deliver value simultaneously.

One of the immediate benefits of the customer survey and segmentation study was the discovery that all customer segments were immune to television advertising. In response to this information, the company eliminated its TV advertising costs without reducing sales. The company also identified four customer segments, each with a distinct buying trigger. It subsequently revised its print and online advertising to appeal to one of the four triggers. Likewise, the company revised its retail store layout to address these four triggers. These small, low-cost changes grew sales much faster and sooner than expected, and bought the CMO the credibility to proceed with the next phase of the customer retention program.

# Case Study: An Agile Conference

It was an exciting time. Interest in agile software development methods was increasing. A group of volunteers banded together to organize one of the first agile development conferences. Because agile methods were still new enough to be perceived as radical, the team believed that it was important for the conference to build a sense of community among the attendees. If the organizers could achieve this goal, then early adopters of agile methods might not feel so isolated. One of the conference organizers, Todd, had built a successful developer conference at his large commercial software company and knew how critical it was for the conference to include social and networking opportunities.

In addition to fulfilling this purpose, the organizers wanted the event to include a sharing of best practices and education. With such a new venture in a new discipline, however, the organizing team was not sure what to expect. They had a passion to deliver and had designed a strong conference program—but there was still enormous uncertainty. Would there be 100 attendees or 500? If there were only 100 attendees, could they afford the social and networking events like an "ice breaker" and a banquet?

Two months before the event, organizers counted up the number of paid attendees—only 69. The team started getting a bit nervous. Should they cancel the ice breaker and the banquet? Should they cut costs even more by printing a cheaper program? How would these changes affect the long-term vision to build the community? The conference chair believed that the ice breaker and banquet were critical; given the choice, he was willing for the conference to lose money if it resulted in a stronger, more connected community. Of course, no one really wanted to lose money on the event. The team was at an impasse: What could they do to resolve the issues stalling the project?

Months earlier, the conference meeting planner had diligently put together a budget. The budget calculated how much money the conference would make or lose based on the number of paid attendees. With just 69 paid attendees, the budget calculation showed that the conference would take a bath, which also meant that the fledgling nonprofit organization of software developers would take a bath. Maybe the prudent thing to do was to cancel any part of the conference that was not absolutely necessary. After all, the organizers had only so much money and needed to fit the conference program into that budget.

While this case seemed to be a purely dollars-and-cents decision, it was, in fact, a dollars-and-cents and *time* decision. Until now, no one had bothered to figure out which decisions needed to be made, and when those decisions needed to be made. Because Todd had experience in organizing conferences for software developers, he turned the static conference budget into a dynamic value model that could be used for decisions.

With this model, the team had to understand some of the possible scenarios and then make some "what if" decisions. They first took an inventory of the existing information. For example, the conference registration form asked participants to indicate which sessions they were planning to attend. A quick analysis of this information indicated several sessions did not have substantial interest. The conference chair made the decision to cancel a couple of these sessions to reduce the size of the program, thereby cutting some costs. Because the purpose of the conference was to build the community, the team recognized that reducing the program by eliminating sessions with low interest was preferable to cutting the social events.

As another example, the team worked with the conference venue to identify which big decisions they could postpone. Along the way, the team members discovered that they did not have to make a decision about the ice breaker or the banquet until a month before the event. This information allowed them to postpone the decisions about the social events until they had better information about registration numbers. One month later, there were enough registrations that the team could safely commit to the social events.

As these examples demonstrate, rather than forcing the team to make decisions based on the static budget, the dynamic value model allowed the team to make the best decisions at the time they needed to be made, and not before. In this case, there was no reason for the urgency to make a decision before more and better information became available.

That first conference had 225 attendees and turned out to be a huge success. The attendees rated the social events as an important part of the conference and one of the reasons they would attend the next conference. The organizers had built and used a value model that relied on key parameters beyond the budget to make decisions. The dynamic nature of the value model made it possible to delay some decisions until more information was available. Once the event started, other decisions could be made in real time. For example, dancing was scheduled to occur after the banquet, but the DJ was hired to work only until 11 P.M. When it became obvious that people were enjoying themselves on the dance floor, it was an easy decision to step up and pay the DJ to extend her time. The remaining participants were most grateful, and spoke very highly of their experience of the event.

The positive publicity from this worked just as expected. The word of mouth spread. Attendees talked about the event with other software developers, and interest in the conference grew. This conference went on to merge with a similar conference in 2005, and the combined conference had 1560 attendees in 2008—a phenomenal growth rate. Although a number of factors contributed to this growth, the conference organizing team was clear that the overall conference experience was critical to their long-term vision for the event.

The organizing team understood the crucial elements of effective decision making. They understood the need to grasp which decisions they had to make, primarily which sessions and other events the conference needed to include. They understood the need to understand when a decision really had to be made, and they were willing to wait until that point to make the decision. For example, in the decision of whether to keep the social events, the organizers understood they needed to know precisely which information was key to this decision—such as the number of registrants, the cost of the social events, the overriding purpose of the event, the terms of payment of the conference location, and attendee preference for sessions. Most importantly, the team used all of this knowledge to generate a valuable result—in this case, a conference that was of the community, for the community, and by the community.

# Decisions and Portfolio Management

You are looking at more than 200 ideas from all over your company. Which ones do you pursue? Which ones do you defer? Which ones do you ignore completely? Which ones do you do first? How are you going to decide? This is the fundamental set of questions associated with portfolio management.

Portfolio management is something that very few organizations do effectively. Organizations typically have too many good ideas. The real challenge of portfolio management is not eliminating bad ideas and projects, although organizations that minimize efforts spent on bad ideas can certainly be more effective. Instead, the real challenge is focusing the organization's efforts on the most important ideas and leaving less important, but still potentially good ideas until later.

Many organizations manage their portfolio in a very ad hoc manner. Others attempt to put a rigorous process in place for financial evaluation and strategic alignment. Unfortunately, all too many attempts to put rigor into the portfolio management process end up spending too much time without achieving any real gain. Because most rely heavily on highly uncertain cost–benefit analysis whose results can be easily gamed, many of these rigorous processes ultimately obfuscate the issue more than they provide clarity. In our experience, keeping things simple and working with the value model provides an excellent framework for managing and having effective conversations about your portfolio. In particular, the tools that we have discussed with regard to purpose, complexity, and uncertainty can be critical factors in portfolio analysis and management.

For example, a government agency was using purpose as a factor in its project portfolio management. The team managers asked the question, "How do we differentiate ourselves?" It turns out that the agency doesn't differentiate itself at all. So how do the managers balance their portfolio of only parity projects? They don't. They realized that there was no real point in putting substantial effort into a portfolio management balancing exercise. A simple approach was sufficient for their needs.

At another organization, a CTO found a need to manage his portfolio of infrastructure projects. All previous attempts to organize and prioritize the portfolio for the steering committee failed. He worked with the decision model and assessed his list of projects based on purpose, uncertainty, and complexity. First the steering committee used purpose to define the IT strategic plan; then they used complexity and uncertainty to assess capability to complete. Along the way, they found ways to reduce uncertainty and complexity and identified capability gaps that needed to be filled before any new projects would be undertaken.

Using these dimensions, the portfolio fell into place in a few hours. The steering committee then prioritized and balanced the list. There were two differentiating projects, but one of the parity projects was an enabler to both. Therefore, the priority was to fill the capability gaps and do the parity project. Only then would the organization take on the differentiating projects. Purpose is not priority: The company and CTO's team now knew what to do. Uncertainty, complexity, and purpose broke the logjam.

## How to Get Started

When we apply the value model, we use the following guidelines and questions to help bring clarity to portfolio investment decisions.

### *Purpose*

Ask yourself these questions about your purpose:

- Which things are you doing or considering doing that are not really mission critical? Can you drop those initiatives?
- In which things are you investing that you could cut the investment to be at parity?
- Which things are currently under parity and need investment just to reach parity?
- Which things are you investing in—or should you be investing in— that will bring your organization a sustainable competitive advantage?

A helpful exercise is to do a gap analysis of the projects against their purpose. The gap analysis results will indicate where you are currently relative to where you would like to be based on your assessment of purpose. Once you have identified the gaps, you can then prioritize projects based on a combination of most critical gaps and the cost to fill those gaps.

### Considerations

Ask yourself about these considerations:

- What are the risk profiles associated with each of the potential projects?
- What are the potential upsides associated with each project?
- What is your capacity to deliver? Do you have the skills necessary to deliver each project in the appropriate time? Do you have the capacity and skills to lead each project?
- Do you have a portfolio with the appropriate balance of project types?
- What are the project dependencies, and how might they affect your overall portfolio?
- What do the market windows look like for your projects? Are some projects time critical and urgent, while others are less so? What would be the consequences of delaying or abandoning a project?
- Which expectations have been set already? If you take action that affects those expectations, what will the consequences be?

Uncertainty and complexity attributes can provide some useful insights, particularly in regard to your organization's ability and capacity to deliver and lead the projects. The primary purpose of investigating these considerations is to surface some issues that are best addressed in conversations. In our experience, the issue of expectation setting and management is often the most critical. The root cause: It is much easier to make promises or set expectations than it is to actually deliver on those promises and expectations. The remedy is to promise no more than necessary and to delay commitments until the last possible moment. This is easier said than done, of course, but enforcing such discipline will pay handsome rewards. Once a promise or expectation is set, the next key is to judiciously manage it and make sure that any issues that would alter the ability to meet those expectations are addressed.

### Costs and Benefits

Identify the costs and benefits:

- Are the cost–benefit indicators so clear that the decision is obvious?
- Which assumptions underlie the cost–benefit analysis?
- What is the band of uncertainty surrounding the costs and the benefits?

Costs and benefits are still important—just don't get hung up on them. If the business case is an overwhelming indicator, then don't spend more time fine-tuning it. Make the decision to proceed or abandon the project and move on. When the decision is not so clear, realize that a variety of assumptions and uncertainties are inherent in the calculations. Spend more time understanding those uncertainties and assumptions than worrying about precision of the cost–benefit analysis.

## How Often to Should You Evaluate the Portfolio?

Our experience has shown that it is more important to evaluate the portfolio regularly than it is to evaluate the portfolio rigorously. That requires keeping the process lightweight, because it is subjected to relatively few criteria. Some complex portfolio scoring models have more 20 scoring criteria and associated weights, all designed to yield a number for comparisons. Having so many criteria merely complicates the process and provides a false sense of rigor. If the process is lightweight, then it is quite reasonable to revisit the portfolio quarterly.

Individual projects should be reevaluated once new information becomes available. The challenge with reevaluation is that oftentimes expectations have been set that may limit or restrict the options that can be considered. For example, in the early stages of the project life cycle, it might appear that a project will be differentiating or supporting the purpose and that the organization has the ability and capacity to deliver. Later, something may change that alters this perception. Perhaps it becomes clearer that the project is not differentiating and needs to be reconsidered as a parity project. Or perhaps what appeared to be relatively easy turns out to be much more complicated. Expectations may have been set that the project will deliver certain results by a specified time, yet we now find that goal to be either a bad idea or an impossible task.

The key is to bring expectations management into the portfolio management process. Stakeholders need to know that decisions will be made in the future that may affect project scoping, delivery, or timing. If funding and delivery occur in an incremental fashion, then we can also use the decision value model to determine when a project should be terminated or when it should end because it has reached the point of diminishing returns.

## Summary

In this chapter, we used cost–benefit analysis where it makes sense. For other decisions, we built a commonsense model that includes critical factors such as purpose and considerations. If we were still uncertain about the "rightness" of our decisions, we identified decisions we can defer and determined how we can deliver value as we gain knowledge to improve the "rightness" of the decision.

For important business, program, and project decisions, the value model is a powerful tool that helps us identify products, services, and productivity improvements. By dividing things into "chunks" of delivery, and then evaluating after every chunk how much value you have and how much value remains to be realized, you will embrace changes in the marketplace. Take a look at the value model again, check the inputs, assess the market readiness and future possibilities in going to market, and then either deliver to the marketplace, stop, or do the next chunk. The more uncertain and nebulous the future, the smaller the chunks.

When you begin to make a decision, go to the value model and begin the conversation.

# CHAPTER 6

# LEADERSHIP "TIPPING POINT"

## The Big Idea

In this chapter, we consider how you can put our tools to work as a leader. Part of your task as a leader is to address the issue of how and when to step back versus how and when to step up without rescuing your teams. We call this the leadership "tipping point."

Leaders can stifle progress when they interfere with team processes. At the same time, they don't want to go over the cliff and deliver the wrong results. Sometimes leaders should stand back and let the team work, and sometimes they should step up and lead. But how do we decide which is which?

## Stepping Back

Let's start with stepping back. You hired your staff members for their abilities to address issues, solve problems, and create innovative and competitive products. You put your people to work improving operations, increasing workflow, and removing bottlenecks. They operate closest to the problems and have the best chance of finding workable solutions. After all, you hired these people to deliver new, exciting, and competitive products to the marketplace before your competition can.

As their leader, you must unleash this talent and allow the team to succeed. Create an environment based on trust; bring together people who have the right knowledge; ensure they understand the objectives, purpose, and constraints of the project—and then step back.

Let's take a look at a case study how a group of leaders put the tools from this book to work so they could step back. Later in the chapter, we provide a process that will enable you to step back. We end with some examples of this process in action.

# Case Study: Leaving Money on the Floor

An architecture firm had an enviable problem: It had more project opportunities than the firm could take on. The projects were theirs, but the market for talent was so tight that the company couldn't get enough people on board. In other words, there was money on the floor and the owners couldn't pick it up. The frustration inherent in this situation was compounded by the fact that all of the firm's owners—the seven principals on the leadership team—could retire in 10 years. The firm was on its third generation of leaders and had a reputation for creating some of the greatest buildings in its area. No one wanted to drop the ball. After all, the company's future success would pad the owners' retirement fund.

"Pollyanna, do you think you can help us?" asked Ken, the president/CEO of the architecture firm. "We are like a seven-headed monster, all going in different directions. What should we do?"

I wasn't sure that this case was a fit for our approach (what you have been reading about in this book). Ken wanted a facilitator for a two-day leadership retreat. I could accept that task—but would it be a waste of our time? I look for leaders who want to take their companies to the next level using our models, not business as usual. I handed Ken a copy of Richard Semler's book, *The Seven-Day Weekend* [2], and asked him to let me know what he thought as I prepared a proposal.

Ken reported, "I got a third of the way through the book and thought this isn't a real company. Then I got on the Internet and found articles about Semler and how he took his company from $12 million to more than $220 million! I'm not sure we can totally turn our company over to the people who work here, but if we want to grow we will need to do things differently. The other partners would like to meet with you before we make a final decision." We set a meeting date and time.

"Are you going to make us create a mission and vision statement?" was their first question.

"No," I replied firmly. "I think that can be a waste of time." I didn't mention that we would revisit the company's purpose and current market position. That would be an exercise during the retreat.

"That's good, because the last time we did one, we spent six weeks working on it and then immediately forgot it."

"Are you going to make us change our leadership styles?" An unusual second question.

"No, I'm not going to make you do anything you don't want to do." I replied tentatively. I know you can't change people. However, I hoped that in the process of working together, if they saw a different way of doing things that required a change in their leadership style, they would consider making the change.

"Each of us would like to spend some time talking to you, Pollyanna, before the retreat."

I set up meetings with each owner and asked the following questions: What's working? What's not working? If you were the president/CEO, what one thing would you do differently? Mostly I listened. All of the owners had something they wanted to tell me. And the meetings were eye opening. Ken was right—the leadership team consisted of seven different people going in seven different directions.

They wanted me to lead their retreat. Ken and I agreed they would address the following questions:

- Which growth rate do we want to sustain?
- Which marketing strategy is needed? (Yes, they would need to continue to fill the pipeline of projects.)
- How can we increase the throughput of projects (both project throughput and organizational productivity)?
- How do we want to handle succession planning—finding potential replacements for the owners, and creating and implementing a leadership transition plan?

## Working Together to Pick Up That Money

We met in the winter, at a very comfortable ski resort.

"I kept hoping all morning that I would not have to go, that an avalanche would come and close the roads. I just didn't want to be there," one of the principals told me later.

The firm's owners thought of themselves as heading in seven different directions. Their company was growing rapidly and they wondered if, by becoming more coordinated in their efforts, they could be more effective. My job was not to find out how to do this, but rather to help them figure out how to work together better.

We began. The principals answered two questions using the collaboration process:

- What's the prize?
- What's getting in your way of achieving the prize?

There were the expected answers for the prize: money, security, creative satisfaction, fulfilling work, and making the decisions. Several responses mentioned developing clients, staff, and themselves.

The obstacles were more revealing. In addition to the usual "not enough time and resources" responses, the principals were aware of their own weaknesses, both as individuals and as a team. Their responses along these lines included "no clear plan," "the urge to do it myself," "team development," "mixing priorities," "not asking for help," "lack of confidence in help/staff/self," and "not wanting to let others down."

Where to begin? We started with something the firm's owners were very familiar with—marketing. They were doing it themselves. Our first step was to look at their differentiation factors.

The principals had two concerns right off the bat: They didn't want to be like the other guys and they didn't want to be a corporate factory. When we took a look at the Purpose Alignment Model, however, we found a mismatch between the real strategy and the way that the company operated.

Measurements (and compensation) were based not on results but on hours "worked"—hours charged to a job, including overtime pay, even if not much work was done. In short, employees were rewarded based on time spent on a project rather the results achieved. The company treated control of overtime hours as a mission-critical attribute and treated project leadership, project tracking, and project and employee support as "who cares" issues.

The company differentiated itself by offering superior designs, but only the principals were trusted with design. This policy led to an obvious conflict with the owners' succession planning and sustainability growth goals.

We then looked closely at the company's growth rate, capacity, and expectations for the future. Over the past few years, the firm had experienced rapid growth, but the architecture business is a very volatile business: Economic swings cause people either to cut back on building or to increase their efforts. Ignoring changes in the marketplace would lead to diminished results. Responding to changes effectively would lead to the slow, but steady growth the firm had experienced in the past. However, if the owners led change, they could continue the higher growth rate they were currently experiencing (see Figure 6.1). Leading change would require all members of the company to step up. But how could the owners do that and still ask employees to increase their project throughput?

"The answers are in your organization," I said. "The members of your organization know what is working, what is not, where the bottlenecks are, and which processes are failing them—and they will know how to fix them." The room was silent. I was, after all, the consultant. I was "supposed" to have answers, not more questions.

"What would that look like?" one of the principals asked.

"We will bring everyone in your organization together in small groups, 25–30 people at a time, and develop strategies and solutions to find ways

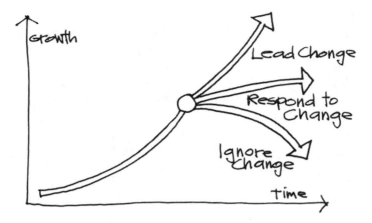

**FIGURE 6.1**   Change versus growth curve

to improve the productivity and throughput in your company." For the architecture firm, that meant four meetings.

---

**AUTHOR'S NOTE**   "Wait, Pollyanna," you are thinking. "We have more than 100 people in our company—a lot more. We can't hold all those meetings and hear from everyone!" As it turns out, four meetings usually are all you need, as long as all interests, levels, and job types in the organization are represented. After these meetings, you will begin to see patterns of the real issues emerge.

---

In these meetings, we addressed four questions:

- What is an open environment? (This was an exercise to have the participants become familiar with using the collaboration process.)
- What is working?
- What is not working?
- How can we fix what is not working?

Prior to these meetings, however, there was more work to be done at the retreat. Before we left the meeting, I asked the seven principals the last two questions. The outcome was interesting and the focus relevant. The owners raised the following topics:

- The need to go faster (do analysis sooner; right-size every phase; increase velocity)

- The need to build a collaborative environment (move from a command-and-control system to collaborative-type leadership; let go of the reins and motivate employees)
- Production leadership (adequate production leadership; adequate guidance for inexperienced staff; track and be accountable for production; manage projects using a forward orientation, not a backward orientation)
- Creation of a place where people want to work (encourage others to help others; accept and acknowledge individuals' unique ways of doing their work; create a creative environment)
- Tools to succeed (in-house training and education; support staff; a mentoring "coach"; field experience to "close the loop" with interns and drafters)

For each item, one of the principals volunteered to develop a strategy, action plans, budget, and exit criteria.

Before the retreat ended, we also talked about a succession plan. Taking attrition into account, the owners would need to select, coach, and mentor 14 potential leaders to replace all 7 principals. Based on the past policy of selecting principals from the senior associates, the pool of possible leaders currently included only two candidates. The president/CEO took on the task of developing a plan for finding, training (when required), and mentoring the next generation of leaders.

The principals looked to the members of their organization to answer questions related to their remaining issues:

- Improve processes (shared ownership process; quality control process; lean processes; follow the same, consistent story; don't reinvent the wheel)
- Improve efficiency (give permission to the person, task, and process; stop doing it twice; gain better control of overtime; give staff room to grow in the firm; no wasted time)
- Be cost-effective (clear, easy tracking; monitor costs and benefits)

From the results of this meeting, we roughly mapped out the firm's Purpose Alignment Model (see Figure 6.2). Its diversity of design was reflected in the company's contracts to build Native American casinos, university buildings, car dealerships, and religious buildings, among others. Its overtime concerns centered on the fact that many employees worked hourly and were paid time and a half for overtime. The owners were concerned about overtime because many principals believed that

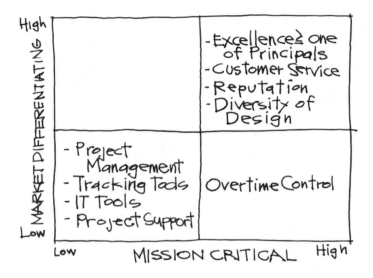

**FIGURE 6.2**    Initial Purpose Alignment Model for an architecture firm

employees were wasting time during their regular hours so they could work the extra hours.

One issue identified as an ongoing problem was the lack of detailed project tracking, IT tools, and project management. Architects led the projects, even though they had no formal training in project management. Instead, learning project management involved on-the-job training—that is, learning as architects worked on projects.

The other people in the organization would now have their chance to identify what they saw as not working and what could be done to improve project throughput. We scheduled the meetings with four groups of employees. After getting past their fears that this would be some "group hugging" event, they understood that they were being asked to identify and solve the problems in their organization. They also decided what they wanted to tell the principals and share with participants in the other team meetings.

The work began. Their insights into what was not working included (in order of their prioritization) the following items:

1. Not enough training
2. Recognition and compensation
3. Lack of leadership

4. Communication
5. Lack of focus on design and design excellence
6. Not enough time
7. Quality issues
8. No empowerment
9. Operational management

Meeting participants developed more than 150 ideas that, when implemented, would solve most of their issues and (ideally) increase their project performance.

One specific issue emerged more consistently than any other: the lack of collaboration on projects with customers and contractors. Architects designed in isolation and then met with the customer to review and get changes. This "revise–review" cycle continued until the customer was satisfied with the design. Members of the firm then met with the contractor to identify what could and could not be done construction-wise to remain within the budget. Based on this information, the "revise–review" cycle began again.

Project tracking was difficult. There were no tools in place to produce enough information to view the status of a project, including time and effort spent and remaining, and estimated due dates. Projects were often run in crisis mode near the committed dates. No resource loading process was in place.

In a meeting of potential leaders to discuss the next steps for the organization, the participants waited for leadership permission to take the next steps. The president/CEO, who was sitting quietly in the back of the room, spoke up: "You want to be leaders, but you are acting like mice."

This event was a cultural turning point. Suddenly people no longer looked to their leaders for answers—they looked to one another. They formed committees based on the results from the team meeting on what was not working and began to implement the solutions they had developed together. When they needed budget allocations, they presented proposals to the principals, who approved valuable efforts. Their first concern was the need to increase their project throughput, so they proposed a set of project management courses.

Project management tools, tracking tools, IT support, and other management tools became mission critical, as the company focused on filling the gaps between its current state and its desired state. To improve project management skills and methods, we trained anyone interested in project management tools, including the Context Leadership Model described in Chapter 4 of this book. We discovered three very large "bull" projects: a

$350 million casino project in Arizona, a combination shopping and residential complex in the heart of downtown, and a university complex in Idaho. The company's "colt" projects consisted of designing interiors in hotel lobbies and other small interior works. "Cow" and "sheepdog" projects were more difficult to differentiate, but we settled on the car dealerships and parking structures as "sheepdog" projects and medical, university, and religious buildings as the "cow" projects.

In the project training classes, teams looked at the "bull" projects and successfully divided them into smaller projects. The university project easily divided into two "cow" projects, and a natural leader emerged to assume one of the smaller efforts. The casino project was also divided into separate projects: The parking structure became a "sheepdog" project, and the restaurants and the hotel became separate "cow" projects. Separating the project components in this way brought all three projects into focus and reduced the risks of complexity and uncertainty as the due date approached.

With the company now measuring its results, managing the amount of overtime worked became a "who cares?" issue (see Figure 6.3). The company hired support staff so that professional staff could focus on design, project management, and customer management. This change in policy created newfound capacity, and the firms' employees began collaborating on projects, designing with customers, and using contractor consultants at every stage of the design.

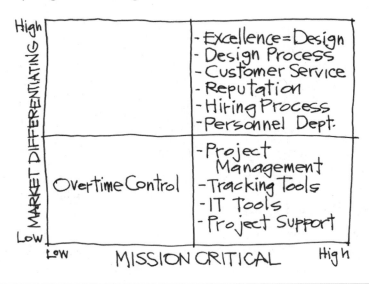

**FIGURE 6.3**  Final Purpose Alignment Model for an architecture firm

## Making Better Decisions

Instead of meeting every week with just the principals, the leaders of the architecture firm began to involve more of the members of their company. Marketing, technology, operations, senior associates, associates, and human resources personnel—all attended various meetings.

The principals also took a closer look at succession planning. Traditionally, the policy had been that only architects could be company principals; these candidates were promoted through the ranks based on the number of years they had worked in the company. This practice was problematic because some architects who were candidates for becoming principals (who had enough years in the company) would be eligible for retirement at the same time as many of the current principals. The owners also realized that many of the potential leaders would not have enough time in the company to serve as principals when they were needed. After this closer look, the current owners began working on how best to expand their principal eligibility policy. As part of this decision, the current principals addressed the "architects only" policy. In the face of the growth of their company, they have begun to realize they need both business leaders and expert project managers. But how do they recognize the value of both types of employees? This is still an open question at this writing.

Traditionally, a major decision for the company has been when to involve customers and contract consultants in the design process. Because customer satisfaction is a major success measurement for an architecture firm, the decisions on when to involve these stakeholders are continuously addressed, resulting in increased throughput and minimal rework.

Pushing decisions on which designs to do, and when, to team members was also a big step. This shift in responsibility gave ownership to the teams as well and took advantage of their expertise to inform the decisions on what to do and by when. On bull projects, team members were able to prioritize these decisions based on their own workload and that of other teams, sharing expertise and finding ways to mentor one another in the process.

## Results and Outcomes

In one year, this company saw a 90% increase in revenues, with a 35% increase in staff, resulting in a nice increase in profits. Most importantly, their customers noticed the difference and customer satisfaction increased.

During a checkup visit, the next-generation leaders were struggling, however. "How do we get our people to work? They do not seem very motivated."

"Use collaboration so that teams understand the company and project goals, and let them decide what they need to do to make the project succeed," was my reply. The ability to choose gave everyone ownership and a stake in creating and contributing to great results. Now everyone stepped up to finish the work and meet deadlines.

At the next retreat, the principals realized that measuring results and being accountable for results built trust. They reviewed the previous year's goals and recognized gaps in succession planning, making specific plans to fill the gaps.

## All This Stuff Is Fine and Good—But Where Do I Start?

One of the most compelling features of these models is that you can apply them immediately. The primary decision filter we use is that our models must be simple to understand and easy to put into use. In this chapter, we have described how we have used these models to solve common problems. And believe us—we face the same problems you do.

As we stated in Chapter 1, there is no "silver bullet" solution to the problems and challenges we all face. However, underneath many of the issues are some common root causes, and the tools described in the book work because they address many of these root causes. These tools will help you and your team to expose the sources of your problems and address them to improve the situation. When you don't understand the root causes, you will likely spend your time and energy dealing with symptoms that show up in everything you do.

Before we work through some mini-scenarios that show how we use the tools, let us first describe our general approach. Because purpose alignment, collaboration, risk analysis, and decision-making processes work so well together, it does not really matter which tool you use first. If you are starting a new project and want to set it and the team up for success, you will want to use the principles of collaboration to convene the right people so that they can define the project purpose, outline the decision-making model, and determine how to mitigate risks. If you want to improve the culture of the team, you will want to build trust as you work through ways to reduce risk, agree on which decisions need to be made and when, and identify the criteria you will use in your decision-making process. If you have been assigned to rescue a troubled or failing project, you can use the tools to discover and prioritize what is working and what is not. Are you trying to make decisions too early or without the right information? Has the team sorted through the complexity and uncertainty risk factors, and assessed the various options for reducing the risks?

In our experience, if your goal is to improve measurable business value, you can start with any one of these tools and see where it takes you and your team. The important thing is to start.

## Pick Any Pain Point

Look around. Where is your organization struggling? Which obstacles keep your company from reaching its corporate goals and objectives? Pick a pain point, any pain point. It could be a goal that was handed down to your team from the executives and that you have no clue how to achieve. Processes or bureaucracy inside your company may be a drag on your teams' productivity. You may need to beat your competition to the marketplace with a new product or service—what should it be? You may have a highly visible project that is so complex you have no idea how to "get your arms around it." Lack of communication, unclear strategy, lack of focus, "Why are we doing this?" questions, chaos, things spinning out of control—pain points can be found in many different areas.

## Convene the Right People

First, convene the right people. Who are the right people? They are the people who want the issue resolved or the project to succeed, the people who are working on the solution, and the people who are in the midst of the problem. Why do this? Because the quality of the solution increases as we involve those both doing and held responsible for the work. This is sometimes the most challenging and frightening thing to do. Some of these people may be angry and bitter. Some may seem clueless about what they want and how they want it. Some may be our biggest critics and think "meetings" are a waste of time. But dive right in. If your problem is a lack of communication, then just convening the right people gets you headed toward a solution.

## Why Do We Care?

Why do you and the members of your group care about this pain point? With the group assembled, get out your sticky notes and pens and use the collaboration process to see what the group believes is the answer to this question. In other words, is this pain point relevant?

## Pick a Starting Point

Next, pick one of the models as a starting point. If your pain point relates to strategy or reasons for doing what we are doing, start with the Purpose Alignment Model. If it focuses on how to organize and approach a project, begin with the Context Leadership Model. If it involves making a decision about what to do and when to do it, then build a value model. If it doesn't fit within any of the models, ask the question, "What's not working?"

## Use the Collaboration Process

Use the collaboration process to decide which model(s) are appropriate. If you start with the wrong model, don't worry. You will probably use all of them at some point. The models are easy to use and you can move through them quickly.

## Mini-Scenarios

As promised, we end this section with some scenarios that demonstrate how we use the tools described in this book.

### Scenario 1: Scope Creep! What Do We Do Now?

What if your pain point is the fact that you are losing control of requirements? Yes, we want to be able to embrace change—and requirements will often change. But how can we make sure we deliver what we need to deliver as our understanding of the problem changes?

Start with the Purpose Alignment Model. Draw and describe the model, and then ask the group to identify which business activities the project supports. Does the project support activities that differentiate, are at parity, are best done through partnership, or are "who cares?" activities? It could be that certain elements of the project need to differentiate while others are at parity. If so, which elements belong where? With that decision in hand, do a gap analysis of what has already been delivered and what is still remaining. These gaps can be both positive and negative. If you have over-invested in a parity element, you would have a positive gap; in that case, it is probably time to either stop work on that element or simplify it. If you have not done enough to either differentiate or get to parity, you have a negative gap to fill.

As you sort through the parts and pieces of the project, bring in the other models. For example, do some of the gaps result from not knowing enough or from making decisions too early? How can you use the uncertainty/complexity model to organize your team and approach to best address those gaps? As the team identifies specific actions you can take to focus the scope of the project, use the collaboration model and have team members volunteer for the work they will own and deliver. Along with this step comes a clear decision about what qualifies as "done." "Done" is when the priority gaps are filled. If it provides any comfort, this approach has always worked for us.

### Scenario 2: Can't We Go Faster?

Everyone wants to increase productivity. But what is the real problem? Doing the wrong things? Constrained bottlenecks? Not enough people? People doing things they are not trained for? This was the case with the architecture firm described earlier in this chapter. We started with the collaboration tool, giving every member of the firm the opportunity to come together in small groups and answer the key questions: What's working? What's not working? How do you want to fix it? In the discussions of what to do, the lack of project management training came up. We then looked at the Context Leadership Model and began moves aimed at helping the company build a better and more manageable project portfolio. Next, we used the Purpose Alignment Model to look at marketing—how the firm could differentiate itself and how it could "sell" that concept.

### Scenario 3: Things Keep Changing!

Change is a problem we all face. In today's highly competitive, interdependent, technology-driven marketplace, change is a way of life. Nevertheless, this statement is not meant to imply that we have to be whipsawed by these changes. If your organization is grounded in strategy—remember that strategy is the same thing as sustainable competitive advantage—you can make rapid decisions and changes that enhance your market position.

Start with the business value model. After convening the right people, analyze the decision-making process in terms of what needs to be decided and when. To address the "what," explore the Purpose Alignment Model to develop your strategically aligned decision criteria. To address the "when," develop a value model conversation to determine the appropriate time to make a decision, a time enabling you to factor in as many changes as possible. You can then compare this decision framework with the Context Leadership Model to find ways to reduce the risks of certain decisions.

## Case Study: Stepping Back

"We have a problem."

Kevin, one of the most trusted members of the team, was nervous while delivering the news. I was the project manager of a controversial, high-profile, and high-stakes technology project being carried out by a diverse cross-section of technical and functional teams drawn from the entire company. Our task list and responsibilities were enormous and highly interdependent. As a team, we went through some early growing pains as we grappled with different personalities, motivations, and backgrounds.

"We have a problem, and the team asked me to talk with you about it."

I was automatically alarmed. I had learned that it took a lot to get Kevin riled and that he had shown an amazing ability to solve a whole host of issues that caused others to panic. If Kevin thought we had a problem, we had a problem.

Kevin sat down across from me and struggled to know how to start. He hemmed and hawed for a few seconds and then said, "We miss you. Over the past few weeks, you have not been involved with us as much as you were earlier. Is there something wrong? Have you been asked to move on to other tasks?"

I immediately calmed down as I realized the problem was with me and not some large or looming problem with the project.

"Kevin," I said, "I apologize for not being a better communicator. There is no problem with you or the team, and I have not been asked to move on to another project. My goal for you and the rest of the project team is not only that we deliver the project, but also that this project prepare you and the other team members for future leadership roles in the company. As you have stepped into and taken charge of your project team roles, I have started to step away from the daily management of the team. I have made a mistake by not telling you about my plans and letting you think that I am becoming disengaged. I would like to fix that right now."

I kept Kevin in my office while I called in the other team members and explained my ulterior plans to them. They were both relieved and anxious—relieved that I was not becoming disengaged from the project and its critical deliverables, but anxious that I expected them to assume stronger leadership roles not just on the project but in the organization as a whole.

It all ended well. After I shared my vision for them with the team members, they actually improved their already outstanding performance. Along the way, I learned two valuable, if unintentional, lessons. The obvious lesson was to better communicate my vision, plans, and expectations to my team members and staff. The more difficult lesson was how, in the future and with different team members, I could repeat my experience of developing this high-performance team. With this team, I had "fallen" into good decisions about how to set up this team for success. Could I leverage this experience into a repeatable process or methodology? As a leader, was I ready to view my role differently and add value through team development rather than by being the source of ideas and guidance?

What do you need to be able to step back? As this story illustrates, you must have a team that you can trust. Without trust, you cannot step back; without your stepping back, your team will not step up to solve sticky business issues and deliver innovative products and services.

## One Last Word

Bring the right people together and ask the question: What's getting in our way of success? Work together, use the collaboration process, and start with any one of the tools described in this book. Listen. Stand back and watch what the group discovers to be the most important barrier. Ask them how they want to remove the obstacles and by when.

# Stepping Up

This last section deals with recognizing how and when to lead.

## How and When to Step Up

There are times when leaders need to step up and lead. As leaders, we want our projects to deliver results, but not just any results, the *right* results—results that are in line with the corporate strategy. You could just lecture team members on this topic and hope they get it. More effective than lecturing, though, is continuously asking questions to help team members discover the answers for themselves: How does this project/feature/objective fit with our company strategy? If it does not, do we need to modify our strategy? Does our prioritization scheme match our business priorities? Can we reach our market window?

## Ask Questions—Reaffirm Ownership

Here's another key to success: Don't take the ownership from your teams—but don't let them flounder for too long, either. It can be difficult to know when the team needs more time to struggle toward a solution and when it needs you to inject some leadership (and not take ownership away from the team). How do you know when to step up? Through your own experience and intuition. If you ask questions rather than simply telling the team members what to do, you will maintain the integrity of the team's own problem-solving process. When you get a sense that team members are thrashing, bring them together. Do not ask what's wrong (this may pass a judgment that they cannot overcome). Do not ask them where they are stuck (they might not be—they might just need a new perspective on the issue). Instead, ask team members to tell you about the project, their approach, their ideas, and their solutions so far. Help them take a new and fresh look at the problem at hand.

When people come into Niel's office looking for a solution, he asks, "What would you like me to do?" Pollyanna asks, "How would you like to solve that?"

This is not easy. When leaders hear a problem and know the answer, they will want to shout out the answer. Once you do this, however, you are cooked: Your effectiveness as a leader diminishes. Suddenly, a steady stream of people will flock to your office, asking you to fix their project and give them the solutions to all their problems. You will have taken away the team's ownership and, in effect, told team members they are incapable of solving their own problems. They will lose pride in their work, and their productivity will drop off dramatically.

When the first Lunar Module was scheduled to go up, the lunar team was doing the last check two weeks before liftoff. They found the gyro—the tool that told the pilots where the module was in three-dimensional space—was drifting, albeit within specifications. To replace it would take two weeks exactly. If anything went wrong, the launch would have to be postponed. After a long discussion, the module team decided to keep the gyro in place. They went to the head project leader and told him of their decision. He asked them one question, "Do you know why the gyro is drifting?" They replaced the gyro—and the launch took place on time.

## When You See Your Own Red Flags

Make a list of the red flags you might see on a project or team. Figure out your tipping point, which determines when you should step up and when you should stand back. There are red flags for both actions! Be sure to identify the red flags that indicate when you should stand back. They can be the hardest ones to detect, recognize, and not act upon (in other words, step back).

Watch for spikes on the complexity and uncertainty graphs. Are they getting better? Hold a meeting and ask questions. To identify other signs that teams might be losing focus, ask these questions:

- How many times are you revisiting the value model?
- Do you have too many differentiating projects?
- Have you got the right leaders on the projects—for example, a "colt" leader on a "colt" project?

## Motivation

People are not motivated by money. That's an interesting statement, but it is also what the research shows. With the architecture firm mentioned earlier in this chapter, the principals were skeptical as well.

"I figure you earn in the mid- to high-six figures per year," I told them in our first retreat meeting. They agreed.

"If I doubled your salary but said that you could not design buildings ever again, would you take it?" None of the seven principals said yes.

What is an effective way to motivate people? Look at what we call "authentic motivation," a concept developed by Alfie Kohn [1]. Kohn states that people are motivated by the three C's: collaboration, choice, and content. We have talked about collaboration in Chapter 3. Give people the choice about what they want to do and how to do it. Okay, we can't always give them the choice of what to do, but we can let them decide on the best way to achieve that "what." Content? People want interesting work.

"Drafting is not interesting work," commented my architect leaders. "But you could involve the people who do drafting in the design sessions and meetings. Perhaps then they could see the value in their work and their contribution to the project. They might also detect errors because now they understand the vision," was my reply.

## Summary

Allow your teams to manage their workload, find solutions, and deliver. Make sure all team members understand that their solutions, objectives, and goals must be in line with the company strategy. Help your teams find their own solutions—but only after they have tried to do so on their own. Don't take ownership of the team's responsibilities. Ask questions without giving answers. Your questions will help your team members discover their own solutions. Use your questions to unleash the talent and creativity in your organization. Then stand back, get out of the way, and let your teams get the "real" work done.

In the stock exchange project, I made only one decision. I knew I was technically too old to have any technical answers; all I could do was to keep the focus. I walked the floor all the time and asked questions. I had no fear about sounding stupid. I cared only about delivering the system to the traders, and I was curious about how the team was thinking.

And the one decision I did make? I let someone go when a team leader came to me and said if I didn't do something, the team would throw him out the window. The team had decided; I just had to go along with it.

## References

[1] Kohn, Alfie. *Punished by Rewards: The Trouble with Gold Stars, Incentive Plans, Praise, and Other Bribes*. Boston: Houghton Mifflin, 1993/1999.

[2] Semler, Ricardo. *The Seven-Day Weekend: Changing the Way Work Works*. New York: Portfolio, 2004.

# CHAPTER 7

# SUMMARY

## Putting These Tools into Action

Now that you have seen some examples of how others have used these tools, this chapter provides you with some quick memory joggers of how to use these tools so that you can apply them in your organization tomorrow—or maybe even today. This chapter includes brief descriptions of the four main tools described in this book, along with some thoughts as to when you can use them and how you can apply them.

## Purpose Alignment Model

This section briefly revisits the Purpose Alignment Model, highlighting what it is, when to use it, and how to use it.

### What It Is

Purpose alignment is a method for aligning business decisions and process and feature designs around purpose. The purpose of some decisions and designs is to differentiate the organization in the market; the purpose of most other decisions is to achieve and maintain parity with the market. Those activities that do not require operational excellence either necessitate finding a partner to achieve differentiation or do not deserve much attention.

In practice, purpose alignment generates immediately usable, pragmatic decision filters that you can cascade through the organization to improve decisions and designs.

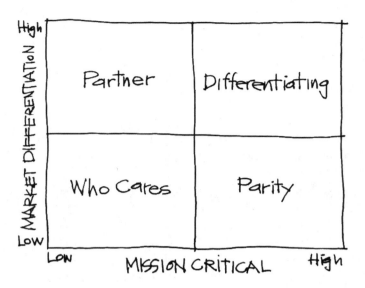

**FIGURE 7.1**   The Purpose Alignment Model, which incorporates strategy intent

## When to Use It

Purpose alignment works well when you need to do these things:

- Define business and IT strategic and tactical plans
- Align IT with business priorities
- Evaluate, plan, and implement large system projects
- Filter and design features and functionality
- Manage project scope
- Reduce resistance to process improvements
- Improve business value by improving focus and resource allocation

## How to Use It

Follow these steps to engage in purpose alignment:

1. Present and explain the model.
2. Identify the business decisions and designs that differentiate your organization.
3. If it helps, you can validate your work using strategy, also known as sustainable competitive advantage, and strategic intent (e.g., cost

leadership, product leadership, best customer solution). Once you have identified the differentiating activities, you should be able to write a simple filtering statement or question that you can use to quickly evaluate future decisions and designs. Before moving on, determine whether any of the differentiating activities can best be delivered via a partnership.

4. Once you have defined the differentiating activities, almost all other activities will fall into the parity category.

5. If you are using the Purpose Alignment Model for strategic and tactical planning, you can next perform a gap analysis on the differentiating, parity, and partnering activities. Your plans should fill the gaps.

6. If you are using the Purpose Alignment Model to design projects, features, and functionality, you can now design around purpose. Design differentiating project elements, features, and functionality to help you win in the marketplace. Design parity project elements, features, and functionality to be good enough. Remember that the parity activities are mission critical and, therefore, cannot be done poorly. Nevertheless, they can be simplified and standardized so long as they deliver operational excellence.

## Leading Collaboration

These sections briefly review our discussion of collaboration.

### What It Is

Collaboration is a powerful tool with which to find the answers in your organization and foster the flow of ideas.

### When to Use It

Use this tool to answer questions as a group, such as when prioritizing projects and determining their purpose, trying to increase productivity and workflow, identifying and developing innovative products and services, and managing risk, uncertainty, and complexity.

## How to Use It

Bring the right people together—those interested in the success of the issue and those affected by the issue. Create an open environment based on trust. Use the collaboration process to stimulate the flow of ideas:

1. Agree to the goal, objective, or problem to be solved.
2. Using sticky notes and marking pens, have each person brainstorm his or her answers, putting one answer on one sticky note and using as many notes as necessary.
3. Have each person read his or her answers aloud to the group while sticking each note on the wall or whiteboard.
4. Ask the entire team to group the notes—in silence. Give them no other directions.
5. As a team, label the groups with an agreed-upon title.
6. Add up the number of groups, divide by 3, and round up. This is the number of votes each person has to select the most important or best solution.
7. Let each person vote next to the title. Make sure participants understand that they can put more than one vote on a group if they feel it has great importance.
8. Tally up the votes.
9. Break up the participants into small teams and have the teams work on ways to implement the groups that received the highest numbers of votes. Each breakout team should take a different group and then report their results to the full team.
10. Work through all relevant groups of solutions.
11. Let the participants decide which tasks they want to do and by when. Stress that they should take on tasks they want to do. Remaining tasks that no one wants to do should be resolved by the full team.

In leading this collaboration effort, remember to use questions to keep the focus; stand back and let people work; trust first; avoid rescuing the team; practice influence, not command and control; over-communicate; and listen.

# Context Leadership Model

These sections provide an overview of using the Context Leadership Model for managing for uncertainty and complexity.

## What It Is

The Context Leadership Model is a method for analyzing projects and/or a portfolio of projects to help project leaders understand how to effectively govern and manage their projects. Uncertainty and complexity are the two dominant characteristics of projects and teams that frame the appropriate project leadership style. This model also deals with issues of leadership development and seeks to discover how to best align leadership styles with projects in a portfolio.

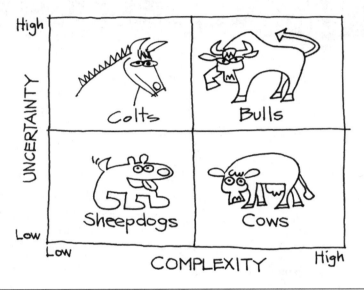

**FIGURE 7.2**   The Context Leadership Model

## When to Use It

The Context Leadership Model is appropriate when tackling the following tasks:

- Determining the effective leadership style for a project
- Identifying potential opportunities to restructure a project so as to lower risk
- Analyzing a portfolio of projects to see whether the overall risk profile is appropriate and/or whether it is in line with the available pool of project leaders
- Developing leadership skills to help project leaders

## How to Use It

Follow these steps to use the Context Leadership Model:

1. Identify the parameters and the scoring that you will use for complexity and for uncertainty. A sample set of parameters and scoring model is summarized in Tables 7.1 and 7.2.

**Table 7.1** Complexity Attributes

| Attribute | Low Complexity (1) | Medium Complexity (3) | High Complexity (9) |
|---|---|---|---|
| Team size | 2 | 15 | 100 |
| Mission critical | Speculative | Established market | Safety critical or significant monetary exposure |
| Team location | Same room | Within the same building | Multisite, worldwide |
| Team maturity | Established team of experts | Mixed team of experts and novices | New team of mostly novices |
| Domain knowledge gaps | Developers know the domain as well as expert users | Developers require some domain assistance | Developers have no idea about the domain |
| Dependencies | No dependencies | Some dependencies | Tight integration with several projects |

**Table 7.2** Uncertainty Attributes

| Attribute | Low Uncertainty (1) | Medium Uncertainty (3) | High Uncertainty (9) |
|---|---|---|---|
| Market uncertainty | Known deliverable, possibly defined contractual obligation | Initial guess of market target is likely to require steering | New market that is unknown and untested |
| Technical uncertainty | Enhancements to existing architecture | We're not quite sure if we know how to build it | New technology, new architecture; may be some risk |
| Number of customers | Internal customer or one well-defined customer | Multiple internal or small number of defined customers | Shrink-wrapped software |

**Table 7.2** Uncertainty Attributes *(continued)*

| Attribute | Low Uncertainty (1) | Medium Uncertainty (3) | High Uncertainty (9) |
|---|---|---|---|
| Project duration | 0–3 months | 3–12 months | More than 12 months |
| Approach to change | Significant control over change | Moderate control over change | Embrace or create change |

2. Score the project and compute the average scores for complexity and uncertainty.
3. Identify the quadrant in which the project falls. Is it a sheepdog, colt, cow, or bull?
4. Look at the attribute scores as in Tables 7.3 and 7.4 to see if any outliers might possibly be altered to lower the score and reduce risk. Common ways to reduce complexity include these options:

- Collocating the team
- Breaking the project into subprojects

Common ways to reduce uncertainty include these options:

- Using of proven technologies
- Reducing project duration and using iterative development

**Table 7.3** Complexity Attributes

| Attribute | Score | Graph |
|---|---|---|
| Team size | 3 | ▮▮▮ |
| Mission critical | 3 | ▮▮▮ |
| Team location | 9 | ▮▮▮▮▮▮▮▮▮ |
| Team maturity | 3 | ▮▮▮ |
| Domain gaps | 3 | ▮▮▮ |
| Dependencies | 9 | ▮▮▮▮▮▮▮▮▮ |

**Table 7.4** Uncertainty Attributes

| Attribute | Score | Graph |
|---|---|---|
| Market uncertainty | 3 | ■■■ |
| Technical uncertainty | 3 | ■■■ |
| Number of customers | 9 | ■■■■■■■■■ |
| Project duration | 9 | ■■■■■■■■■ |
| Change | 3 | ■■■ |

5. If you are considering breaking a project into subprojects, remember to look for strong cohesion within projects and loose coupling across projects.
6. Use Table 7.5 to match the project to a leader with an appropriate leadership style suitable for the project according to the uncertainty and complexity mapping.

**Table 7.5** Project Leadership Styles for Different Project Types

| Project | Project Leader | Practices |
|---|---|---|
| Sheepdog | Novice or no explicit leader | Just the core practices that you wish to have for all projects |
| Colt | Technical or business lead | Short iterations with continuous feedback |
| Cow | Seasoned project manager | Structured project plans with appropriate documentation |
| Bull | Mentor | Iterations and feedback to deal with uncertainties and appropriate structure to deal with the complexity |

## Value-Based Decision Making

These sections provide a review of value-based decision making.

### What It Is

Value-based decision making is a method for making critical organizational decisions in an informed and timely manner. Teams using this tool identify the most critical decisions they face, determine when they need to make those decisions, and figure out which information they need to best make those decisions.

Because critical decisions often directly affect the value generated or lost by an organization, it is helpful to organize the necessary information in the form of a value model; this model can be created in a collaborative manner and revisited when the team gets new information. Figure 7.3 shows the value model, including how it organizes the key information needed for decision making.

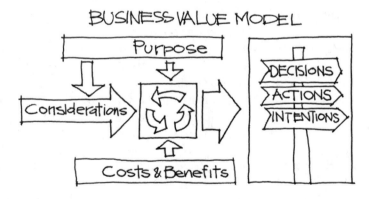

**FIGURE 7.3** The value model

## When to Use It

Value-based decision making is appropriate when tackling the following tasks:

- Determining which products to enhance, maintain at the current status, or stop supporting
- Determining which projects to start
- Determining which projects to continue
- Determining which projects to stop

## How to Use It

Follow these steps to implement value-based decision making:

1. Identify the critical decisions facing your organization that warrant an extra bit of scrutiny and analysis. Select decisions where the effects of a decision outweigh the costs incurred to reach it using this approach.
2. Determine when these decisions need to be made. This time frame is usually based on when options become no longer available, or when the cost of a delayed decision outweighs the value derived from making the decision.
3. Determine the information required to make an informed decision. Define the purpose, considerations, costs and benefits.
4. Use the time until the decision needs to be made to gather the information identified in step 3. Organize this information in the form of a value model so that you are able to revisit your decision when the inputs change.
5. When you have gathered all of the necessary information, or when the time to decide arrives, make the decision based on optimal value delivery to the marketplace.
6. Implement the decision as effectively and efficiently as possible.
7. Repeat the decision-making process regularly, especially when conditions change.

# INDEX

## A

acquisition example (value model inputs), 99

additional information needs in decision making, 104-105

agile conference planning example (decision making), 115-117

alignment of purpose. *See* Purpose Alignment Model

analytics, as differentiating activities, 30

Apple iPhone example (customer expectations), 104

architecture company example
collaboration, 39
leadership tipping point, 124-133
motivation, 140

asking questions as leader, 60, 139

autonomy, 49

## B

Bennis, Warren, 47

Berra, Yogi, 76

Boeing 777 example (team assembly for collaboration), 49-50

Bohr, Niels, 76

bull projects (context leadership model), 71-72
leadership development, 89-92

software product development example, 87-89

splitting into subprojects, 80-84

business strategy. *See* purpose

## C

change, approach to, evaluating project uncertainty, 76

change example (leadership tool starting points), 136

changes versus growth, architecture company example, 126-127

collaboration, 7-8, 39-43, 145-146
architecture company example, 125-131
implementing, 63-65
leading, 53-63
asking questions, 60
failure, learning from, 61
focus, maintaining, 60-61
measurement based on results, 61-62
organizational direction, 58
standing back, 58-60
team assembly, 53-56
trust, importance of, 56-57
unprofessional behavior, ignoring, 62-63
model selection, 135
pain points, determining, 134

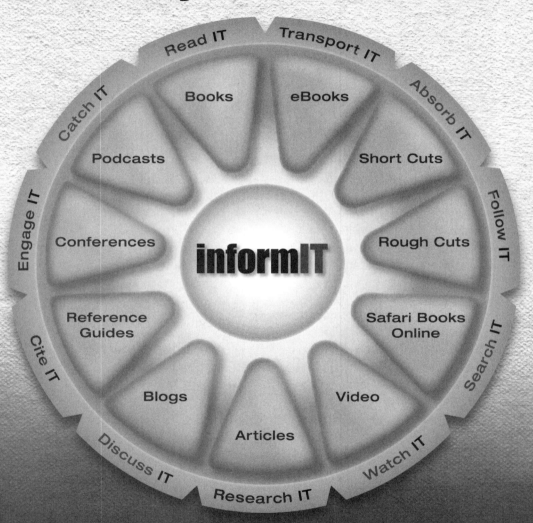

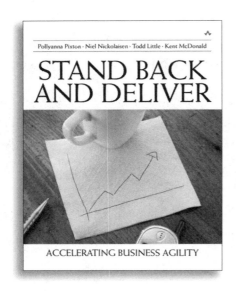

**FREE Online Edition**

Your purchase of **Stand Back and Deliver: Accelerating Business Agility** includes access to a free online edition for 45 days through the Safari Books Online subscription service. Nearly every Addison-Wesley Professional book is available online through Safari Books Online, along with more than 5,000 other technical books and videos from publishers such as Cisco Press, Exam Cram, IBM Press, O'Reilly, Prentice Hall, Que, and Sams.

**SAFARI BOOKS ONLINE** allows you to search for a specific answer, cut and paste code, download chapters, and stay current with emerging technologies.

## Activate your FREE Online Edition at www.informit.com/safarifree

> **STEP 1:** Enter the coupon code: RJWOGBI.

> **STEP 2:** New Safari users, complete the brief registration form.
> Safari subscribers, just log in.

If you have difficulty registering on Safari or accessing the online edition, please e-mail customer-service@safaribooksonline.com